Howard Hillman's Kitchen Secrets

KHOWARD HILLMAN'S KITCHEN SECRETS

by
Howard Hillman

editorial/research project director:
Janet Roberts

special research:
Pearl De Francesco
Cherry Dumaual

A Bobbs-Merrill Book
MACMILLAN PUBLISHING COMPANY
New York
COLLIER MACMILLAN PUBLISHERS
London

Macmillan Publishing Company
866 Third Avenue, New York, N.Y. 10022
Collier Macmillan Canada, Inc.

Designed by Edward Smith Design, Inc.

Library of Congress Cataloging-in-Publication Data
Hillman, Howard.
Howard Hillman's Kitchen secrets.
1. Cookery.   I. Title.   II. Title: Kitchen secrets.
TX651.H55   1985   641.5   85–9674
ISBN 0–02–551610–8

Macmillan books are available at special discounts for
bulk purchases for sales promotions, premiums, fund-raising,
or educational use. For details, contact:
Special Sales Director
Macmillan Publishing Company
866 Third Avenue
New York, N.Y. 10022

10   9   8   7   6   5   4   3   2   1

Printed in the United States of America

**To the discoverer
of the world's first cooking tip***

* I suspect the discoverer was a hungry caveman
who, one fine evening, accidentally dropped
a piece of raw meat into his campfire,
tasted the flavorful results
and spread the good news

INTRODUCTION

"What, another cooking tip book?" you may ask. Granted, many exist, but most are marred with questionable if not erroneous advice. Consider, for instance, this sampling from one of the leading cooking tip books:

> "5 tablespoons plus 2 teaspoons equal ⅓ cup."
> "The safest place to store knives is on magnetic holders."
> "Canned butter is absolutely delicious."
> "Try adding instant coffee powder to a gravy for a really nice flavor."

For the record, 5 tablespoons plus *1 teaspoon* equals ⅓ cup; knives occasionally fall off magnetic holders; canned butter is dreadful; instant coffee powder lends a horrendous flavor.

I trust you will find the tips in this book to be reliable. If your answer is "yes," my staff and I have accomplished our goal.

These are the tips that I have been collecting, discovering, and kitchen testing over the years. I've been passing them on to my friends and now, with this book, I can share them with you, too.

The tips encompass a variety of culinary steps, from shopping to cooking to using leftovers. They are the type of pointers that will increase your cooking skills and enjoyment.

Naturally, I would be delighted if you would share the tips with your friends. The more people who can take advantage of them, the better.

INTRODUCTION

    Should you have any cooking tips you wish to share with me, please send them to me in care of my publisher. I am always eager to learn new culinary tricks and I will be happy if you share yours with me.

—Howard Hillman

Howard Hillman's Kitchen Secrets

A

ABALONE

☐ For optimum tenderness: choose relatively small abalones; slice the flesh into ¼-inch-thick slices and pound them into ⅛-inch-thick slices with a flat mallet or the back of a heavy cast-iron skillet; do not pound the slices to more than half their original thickness, because excess pounding will make the meat tough again; sauté the pieces in a combination of butter and oil for no more than 40 seconds for the first side and 20 seconds for the second.

ACIDULATED WATER

☐ When a recipe calls for acidulated water to keep the exposed flesh of a cut or peeled fruit or vegetable from turning brown, use a mixture comprising 1 tablespoon of vinegar (or 2 of lemon juice) per quart of cool water.

ACORN SQUASH

☐ Lift the squash. Buy it only if it is heavy for its size.
☐ The rind should be hard and free of cuts and soft spots.
☐ The rind will dry out when baked unless you rub it with oil or butter.
☐ When baking the squash whole, pierce the rind in several places to let excess internal steam escape.

À LA MODE

☐ Always use a high grade ice cream when topping a slice of hot pie. A mediocre ice cream will melt too quickly and water-log the piecrust.

ALCOHOL

☐ Alcohol has a lower boiling point than water and is, therefore, more apt to splatter when you add it to hot oil in a pan. Therefore, add only a tablespoon of the alcoholic beverage at a time, particularly if you're using a high-content spirit like gin.

☐ Air is wine's worst enemy. Therefore, transfer the leftover contents of a bottle of wine into a smaller container, one just barely large enough to hold the leftover wine. This minimizes the airspace inside the bottle.

☐ *See also* Flambéing.

AL DENTE

☐ Pasta is not the only food that should be cooked al dente (just to the point where some resistance still remains when you bite into the food). Rice, bulgur wheat, and other cereal grains should be cooked al dente, too, so as not to be mushy.

ALLSPICE

☐ Buy an extra peppercorn mill for storing and grinding your whole dried allspice berries.

ALMONDS

☐ To skin almonds, put them in a bowl, cover them with boiling water, and let them stand for 2 minutes. Drain and press the nuts between your thumb and index fingers, popping the nutmeats out of their skins. Then spread them on a baking sheet and dry them in a preheated 325-degree oven for several minutes.

ALUMINUM FOIL

☐ It's best not to store high acid foods, such as orange sections or leftover veal piccata, in aluminum foil. Acid reacts chemically with aluminum, giving the food an off flavor. (If you unwrap the food and the foil has a powdery white discoloration, damage to the veal has already taken place.)

☐ Placing aluminum foil over a roasting turkey or chicken may help to keep the meat from drying out, but this widely used cooking technique also makes the meat mushy. In effect, you are steaming, not roasting, the bird. If drying out is a problem, baste the bird more frequently.

ANCHOVY PASTE

☐ Give your leftover fish and meat sauces new life by blending a dab of anchovy paste into them.

ANISE SEEDS

☐ Fennel seeds or star anise may be substituted for anise seeds. All have a similar licorice flavor.

APPLES

Marketplace Pointers

☐ The skin should be clean, smooth, and of a vivid hue for its variety. Examine the fruit closely for bruises, decay, worm holes, and other blemishes.

☐ Avoid waxed apples if you plan to eat the skin. (The wax coating is edible but prevents you from washing away foreign substances like pesticides that may be trapped between the wax skin layers.)

HOWARD HILLMAN

☐ The best test for ripeness is to sniff the apple. If you can't smell the characteristic appley aroma, the fruit is probably unripe (or immature). However, if the scent smacks of fermented cider, the fruit is likely over the hill.

☐ If you plan to eat the apple raw, it should be ripe. An unripe one hasn't reached its flavor peak and contains indigestible starch.

☐ If you plan to cook the apple, you need extra tartness and firmness. Therefore, the fruit should be slightly underripe. There is no need to be concerned about the indigestible starch because heat makes it palatable.

☐ The best apples for baking whole or in pieces are the cooking apples. The crab, Rhode Island Greening, Rome Beauty, and York Imperial head the list. Of these four, the Rome Beauty is best for baking whole and the Rhode Island Greening for pie-making.

☐ All-purpose apples can be used for eating raw or, if cooking apples are unavailable, for cooking. Among the best all-purpose varieties are Baldwin, Cortland, Granny Smith, Gravenstein, Grimes Golden, Jonathan, Lady, Macoun, McIntosh, Newtown Pippin, Northern Spy, Stayman, Wealthy, Winesap, and Yellow Transparent. Of these, the Granny Smith is tops.

☐ The Cortland is a good salad apple because its bright white flesh does not turn brown readily.

☐ The two worst apples are the red and golden Delicious, America's two best sellers. They lack sufficient tartness to balance their sweetness. And, except for that sweetness, they are relatively bland. Also, there is little texture to excite your palate after the initial crisp bite.

Kitchen Hints

☐ Carbon steel knife blades cause apples to turn brown. Always cut apples with a stainless steel or other non-corrosive knife blade.

☐ There are several methods to keep the air from turning the freshly cut surfaces of apples brown: Store the apple pieces partially submerged in a little orange or pineapple juice; completely submerge the pieces in double-strength acidulated water (1 tablespoon of lemon juice or ½ tablespoon of vinegar per cup of water); soak the apples in a solution of ¼ teaspoon salt per cup of cool water.

☐ If you're making a salad containing oranges, simply toss the apple pieces with that acidy fruit. Coating the apple pieces with vinaigrette sauce or mayonnaise also does the trick.

☐ Tried and proven companions: brown sugar, cabbage, caraway seeds, cheese, cinnamon, cloves, cranberries, cream, lemon juice or rind, nutmeg, nuts, onions, pork, prunes, raisins, and rhubarb. Children love apple slices smeared with peanut butter and/or honey.

☐ Sugar helps maintain the shape of apple pieces as they cook. Therefore, unless you are making a purée like applesauce, it makes sense to incorporate the sugar at the beginning of the cooking process.

☐ Equivalents: Three medium-sized apples equals 1 pound; 2 to 3 pounds are needed for a 9-inch pie.

☐ *See also* Apple Pie, Fruit, and Waxed Fruits and Vegetables.

APPLE PIE

☐ If you are baking a pie with all-purpose rather than cooking apples, make two adjustments in the recipe: Cut the pieces a little larger than usual to keep the cooking fruit from disintegrating; and add a little lemon juice to give the pie the necessary tartness to balance its sweetness.

☐ *See also* Apples.

APRICOTS

☐ Buy apricots that are fresh-fragrant and golden in hue.

☐ Once ripe, the apricot is especially susceptible to decay

and bruising, so be sure to examine each apricot closely for possible discoloration, soft spots, and other defects before taking them home. Store this fruit where it cannot be jolted or bumped accidentally.

☐ *See also* Fruit and Waxed Fruits and Vegetables.

ARTICHOKES

☐ Artichokes are at their best in springtime.

☐ The leaves (scales) should cling tightly to the body and be firm and intensely green.

☐ Generally, the smaller the artichoke, the more tender it will be.

☐ Dirt easily hides between the leaves. Before cooking the artichoke whole, hold it by its stem end and plunge it up and down vigorously in cold water for about 15 seconds.

☐ To keep the exposed flesh of a cut or trimmed artichoke from turning brown because of oxidation, submerge the vegetable in acidulated water (1 tablespoon of vinegar or 2 tablespoons of lemon juice per quart of water) until you are ready to cook it.

☐ For the same reason stated above, cook artichokes in water spiked with vinegar or lemon juice.

☐ Your artichokes will acquire an unappetizing gray tone if you cook them in a pot made of a corrosive material, such as iron or aluminum. Instead, use a stainless steel, Teflon-lined, or other non-corrosive utensil.

ASPARAGUS

Marketplace Pointers

☐ April and May are the peak months for asparagus.

☐ If the bud cluster at the tip of an asparagus isn't compact, it's over the hill.

☐ Ideally, the exterior should be green from the tip to the bottom of the stalk.

☐ Examine the cut base. If it is woody or otherwise dried out, you can be sure that the asparagus was harvested too long ago.

☐ The stalk should be semi-rigid, not limp.

☐ Straight stalks are preferable to curved ones.

Kitchen Hints

☐ For the sake of even cooking, select stalks with reasonably identical diameters.

☐ Stop cooking asparagus before they become limp and lose their bright green color.

ASPARAGUS VINAIGRETTE

☐ Buy and cook twice as much asparagus you need for a meal. While the asparagus are still steaming hot, marinate the surplus supply in a vinaigrette sauce, cover, refrigerate it, and enjoy as a ready-to-eat cold appetizer in a day or two.

AU GRATIN DISHES

☐ Give leftover meats and vegetables a new twist by turning them into an au gratin dish. The technique is relatively easy. For instance, cut leftover cauliflower into small pieces, coat them with a white sauce, and transfer the mixture to a greased baking dish. Top with ⅛-inch layer of bread crumbs, mixed with grated cheese, if you like. Heat the preparation in a preheated 350-degree oven until the crumbs turn brown.

AVOCADOS

☐ Avocados are at the height of their season from February to April.

HOWARD HILLMAN

☐   The fruit should feel heavy for its size.

☐   Most avocados on the market require several days of ripening in your home, so plan ahead.

☐   If you're buying the avocado for immediate consumption, it should be enticingly fragrant and feel slightly soft. A noticeably soft specimen will be past its prime; a wood-hard one will never ripen properly.

☐   To hasten ripening, store the avocado at room temperature in a pierced paper bag. (The ripening process will be even faster if you also place an apple in the bag, because that fruit gives off the avocado-ripening ethylene gas.)

☐   Use a stainless steel rather than a carbon knife to cut avocado, because the carbon chemically interacts with the avocado flesh, giving it a blackish tint.

☐   To retard oxidation (which will turn the freshly cut surfaces of an avocado brown), coat the exposed flesh with lemon or lime juice. Then cover the storage container with its lid or plastic wrap.

☐   Leftover avocado purée or pieces will not brown as readily if you store the avocado pit with them.

B

BACON

Marketplace Pointers

☐   If you fry bacon frequently, consider buying a square frying pan or, for a large family, a rectangular griddle. They are more suitably shaped than round pans.

☐   Buying bacon that has more lean than fat is counter productive, because fat gives the bacon most of its desirable flavor and crispness. A three-to-two fat-to-lean ratio is optimum. If you are concerned about the extra fat, remember that most of the fat is rendered during the cooking process.

☐   There is a direct correlation between the thinness of a slice of bacon and how crisp it fries.

☐   Presliced bacon is convenient, but slab bacon costs less, stores longer, and usually has more flavor.

☐   Sliced bacon should never be exceptionally limp or coarse-grained. Moldiness and dullness are also bad signs.

Kitchen Hints

☐   Sliced bacon will stay fresh for only up to a week in the refrigerator once you open its vacuum pack.

☐   Nitrate-free bacon is a boon for the health-conscious consumer, but it has a very short storage life. Use it within several days of purchase.

☐   Bacon does not freeze well. Its high salt and fat content prevent successful long-term freezing. In addition, the freezing process creates ice crystals that cause splatter when the bacon fries.

☐   Bacon tends to rip and stretch if you pull the slices apart when they are still refrigerator cold. Bring the bacon to room temperature (allow 30 minutes) before attempting the chore.

☐ Your bacon will be crisper, and you will reduce splatter if you pour off the fat as it accumulates during the frying process.

☐ To minimize splattering and shrinking, start frying the bacon in a cold pan—and cook it over moderate rather than high heat. Lower the heat at the first sign of smoke.

☐ Burnt bacon is inimical to your health. It's carcinogenic.

☐ Substituting artificial bacon bits for real bacon gives your preparation a chemical flavor. If you don't have genuine crushed fried bacon on hand, substitute some other flavoring agent, such as minced ham.

BAKED POTATOES

☐ For effective baking, use the dry and mealy Idaho or other russet potatoes, because new potatoes are too waxy and moist.

☐ Baking a potato wrapped in aluminum foil produces more of a steamed than a baked potato, because the foil traps the moisture escaping through the skin.

☐ Don't rub the potatoes you are about to bake with butter or oil: You want a crisp skin to contrast with the fluffy flesh.

☐ Placing a large nail or other metal spike through a potato will shorten its baking time but will allow too much steam to escape, ruining the texture of the potato.

☐ However, you must allow a small amount of steam to escape for the sake of texture and for preventing a possible explosion. Pierce the skin 1 inch or so deep in several places with the tines of a fork before placing the spud in the oven.

☐ The easiest and most traditional way to serve a baked potato is to blossom it. Use the tines of a fork to cut out a deep, elongated "X" on the top of the potato. Then, using your fingers, squeeze up some of the white flesh. Top with butter or a sauce.

☐ A visually interesting variation of the baked potato is the roasted concertina potato. First you create an "accordion" by cutting it crosswise on the length into ¼-inch-thick slices without cutting completely through the spud. (To do this, place the handles of two wooden cooking spoons on both sides of the potato.) Once cut, brush the exposed flesh with a herb and melted butter mixture, being careful not to break the spud apart. Bake in a preheated 400-degree oven for 45 minutes. To prevent scorching, baste the flesh every 15 minutes.

☐ *See also* Potatoes.

BAKING

☐ Reduce the oven setting called for in a recipe by 25 degrees when baking in a glass pan. Reason: Food cooks faster in glass than it does in metal.

☐ Piecrusts will not brown properly if you use a shiny pan. To brown a crust, use a glass or dull-finished baking pan because it, unlike the shiny variety, does not reflect the heat.

☐ Removing ramekins and custard cups from the oven with pot holders or a spatula is clumsy at best. A quick and efficient way is to use your bare fingers. You won't get burned if you briefly soak your fingers in ice water, pat them dry with a towel, and then immediately and quickly transfer the vessel from the oven to a heat-proof surface.

BAKING POWDER

☐ Baking powder gradually loses its potency as it sits on your shelf. An opened tin should stay fresh for about six months if you keep it tightly sealed. Common sources of the debilitating moisture include wet measuring spoons and steaming kettles.

☐ You can easily determine whether you need a fresh supply by conducting this simple chemical experiment in your kitchen: Pour ¼ cup of hot tap water over ½ teaspoon of baking powder. If this mixture doesn't bubble actively, your dough or batter will not properly rise.

☐ Out of baking powder? Substitute ½ teaspoon of baking soda (sodium bicarbonate) and a pinch of cream of tartar for each teaspoon of baking powder.

☐ Don't incorporate baking powder into a batter or dough too early. Otherwise, much of its leavening power will have been lost by the time the preparation is cooked. For the same reason, don't overbeat or overknead dough. With pancake batter, for instance, it is not necessary to have a perfectly smooth mixture. The small lumps should disappear by the time the pancakes reach the diner's plate.

☐ If you're making buttermilk pancakes or biscuits, use baking soda instead of baking powder. Otherwise, the leavening process will be hindered and the food will have too much of an acid taste.

☐ Measure baking powder accurately. Your baked items will be heavy if you are too conservative and bitter if you are too liberal with this leavening agent.

BANANAS

☐ Don't buy a banana if its stem end is cut too close to the fruit. The banana will spoil quickly because its flesh is exposed to the air.

☐ Plump bananas ripen better than thin ones.

☐ Ripen a banana before eating it. Otherwise, its indigestible starches won't convert to digestible sugars.

☐ The banana will be optimally sweet when brown flecks begin to appear on the yellow peel. (These markings indicate ripening, not decay.)

☐ Sharing a banana with a friend? As long as the fruit is not overripe, you can easily snap it in half with your hands—and there will be no knives or cutting board to clean. Try it with your next banana. Just be sure to divide the fruit with a sharp snap rather than a slow squeeze.

☐ Citrus juice or other acid will keep a peeled banana from turning brown.

☐ Though you want a ripe banana for eating out of hand, you need a slightly unripe one for cooking, because it will better keep its shape when subjected to heat. The cooking process, incidentally, will make the indigestible starches edible.

BARBECUE

☐ Cheap briquettes are seldom a bargain. They burn much quicker and with less intensity than quality ones, and, consequently, you usually end up spending more because you have to buy more of them.

☐ Never stack the unlit coals densely. Create a pyramid or cone mound, because the more air space there is between the individual coals, the sooner they will be ready for cooking.

☐ Melting fat causes flare-ups, so trim the excess fat off beef, lamb, or pork before barbecuing. To prevent flare-ups when barbecue-roasting a fatty hunk of meat or whole chicken, place a drip pan in the middle of the coals directly underneath the meat.

☐ Don't brush a barbecuing chicken with a sugar-rich barbecue sauce until the last 15 minutes of cooking. Sugar scorches, giving the food a burnt flavor and appearance. If you marinate the chicken in a sugary sauce, brush or wipe it off before barbecuing.

☐ Experiment with adding other aromatic substances besides hickory chips to your coals. Have you tried dried thyme or rosemary, for instance?

☐ Don't place the food on the grill until the briquettes stop flaming. Otherwise, the flames will scorch the meat's exterior.

☐ The coals are sufficiently hot for barbecuing steaks and hamburgers as soon as it becomes unendurable to hold your outstretched hand 1 inch above the grill for at least 3 seconds.

☐ Don't crowd the food on the grill. Leave at least 1 inch of space between the pieces. Your food will be crisper and more evenly cooked.

☐ Fish requires a lower heat intensity than chicken, hamburgers, and steaks.

☐ Make "barbecued potato planks" by slicing baking potatoes lengthwise into ½-inch-thick planks. Then brush their skins and flesh with a butter, herb, and pepper mixture. Reassemble and wrap each potato in aluminum foil. Bury the potatoes in hot coals for approximately 40 minutes.

☐ To test steaks for doneness without using a thermometer, press the meat with your index finger. The meat is rare as soon as you detect some springyness. If the surface feels crusty and unyielding, the meat is well done.

☐ Always tightly seal an opened bag of briquettes. If the briquettes absorb moisture from the air, they will burn less readily.

BARBECUING EQUIPMENT

☐ Don't economize on a barbecue unit: If the metal is thin gauged or shoddily welded, the bottom may fall out sooner than you expect. Should you already own a thin-gauged unit, line it with foil to minimize the effect of the fiery heat on the metal.

BASIL

☐ Fresh basil leaves should be a vivid green and not wilted or mottled with dark spots.

☐ Dried basil should not be considered a substitute for fresh basil, because they have different aroma, flavor, and texture profiles. You can't make pesto sauce from dried basil. Nonetheless, dried basil is a worthy herb in its own right.

BAY LEAVES

☐ A bay leaf, at its best, is whole and pliable, not broken or brittle. Ignore any with brown specks or a faded hue.

☐ Given a choice, choose squat rather than elongated bay leaves.

☐ Sniff a few bay leaf samples; they should have a fresh, characteristic aroma.

☐ The flavor of a bay leaf may overwhelm a slow cooked dish if that herb is left in the pot for the entire cooking time. Thirty minutes, more or less, is the ideal.

☐ Always remove a bay leaf from a dish before you serve it. There are many instances of diners accidentally swallowing a sharp-edged piece. Moreover, even though the flavor components of the leaf are safe to digest, the solid leaf per se is unwholesome if consumed in more than a small quantity.

BEAN CURD (TOFU)

☐ If a market stores its fresh bean curd in a water bath and allows its customers to reach into it with their hands, don't buy their bean curd. Pathogenic microorganisms flourish in a bean curd-water environment.

☐ Refrigerate fresh bean curd submerged in water in a covered jar or bowl. If you change the water every day, the bean curd should stay fresh for several days.

☐ Bean curd makes an excellent addition to many dishes. It provides color and texture contrast.

☐ Tofu provides variety in another way; it tastes slightly different with each recipe, because it easily absorbs the flavor of the other ingredients.

☐ Japanese-style bean curd has a more delicate texture than

the Chinese version. It is ideal for soups and gently tossed salads. For the more vigorously concocted preparations, such as stir-fried dishes, use the Chinese-style tofu.

☐   Here's a tip for calorie-counters: Purée bean curd in a food processor and use it in place of cream in soups.

BEANS (DRIED)

Marketplace Pointers

☐   Be sure a bean has its characteristic color. Faded beans indicate improper or prolonged storage.

☐   If you see pinholes on a bean, it has been attacked by bugs.

☐   Canned preprocessed beans may be a convenient time-saving substitute for dried beans, but you sacrifice considerable texture and flavor.

Kitchen Hints

☐   Always examine beans closely for possible pebbles and other foreign matter before you soak and cook them. If they are not removed, a diner could break a tooth.

☐   Don't mix two batches of beans, even if they are of the same variety. Reason: Should one of the batches have been stored for an appreciably longer time, it will be drier and, therefore, will require a longer cooking time.

☐   For best results, soak beans overnight. If you forget to plan ahead and are willing to sacrifice a little flavor and texture, use the quick-soak method. Cover the beans with cold water and bring to a boil. Then simmer for 5 minutes and turn off the heat. Let the beans soak for 2 hours before you start the cooking process.

☐   A bean's degree of hardness will determine how long you should soak and cook it. The harder the bean, the longer the required time. Relatively hard beans (the soybean, navy bean, black bean, and pinto bean, for instance) require overnight soaking and up to 3 hours cooking. Relatively soft beans (including lentils and split peas) require no soaking or a minimum soaking time and ¾ to 1½ hours cooking time.

☐ Select an amply large bowl for soaking beans. During the reconstitution stage, they usually more than double in size.

☐ To minimize flatulence, change the soaking water several times and cook the beans in fresh water.

☐ Simmer, don't boil, beans—for the sake of tenderness and texture.

☐ Salt chemically toughens beans as they cook. Therefore, salt the preparation only during the final half hour of cooking time.

☐ To tell if your beans are adequately cooked, cut one in half and examine its center for a chalky interior. The beans are ready to eat as soon as their chalky interior disappears.

☐ Another test for doneness is to blow on several samples in a spoon. If their skins split, the beans are ready to eat.

BEATEN EGG WHITES

☐ First rule: Egg whites should be at room temperature before beginning the beating process.

☐ If possible, put off beating egg whites on a muggy or damp day. Moisture-laden air partially collapses the beaten egg whites.

☐ A pinch of cream of tartar helps stabilize beaten egg whites. Whipping the eggs in an unlined copper bowl with a metal whisk does the same, because of the generated electrostatic force.

☐ You won't be generating much electrostatic force, however, if your bowl is not pure copper. Most of the copper bowls sold today are alloys.

☐ The worst type of bowl for beating egg whites is made of plastic, to which grease tenaciously clings.

☐   The best way to beat egg whites is to start at a slow speed and to gradually increase the pace. If you were to begin the process at a fast speed, you would create large and, therefore, unstable bubbles.

☐   Whip egg whites in a thoroughly clean and greaseless bowl, as even a speck of egg yolk or fat will keep the beaten egg whites from reaching their full potential volume.

☐   Should a speck of yolk accidentally fall into the bowl containing the egg whites, remove it with a Q-tip or with one of the sharp edges of a broken eggshell.

BEEF

Marketplace Pointers

☐   The closer the cut's anatomical location to a hoof, horn, tail, or belly, the less tender it will be.

☐   The meat of an older animal is tougher than that of a younger one.

☐   The best USDA grade is Prime. Choice is the runner-up.

☐   The most tender sirloin steak is the one that is cut from directly next to the porterhouse steak. To identify this cut from the various other sirloin steaks, look for the one that most closely resembles the shape of the porterhouse steak.

☐   For the best value, buy the porterhouse steak with the largest tenderloin muscle and the smallest tail (the tough belly part of the cut).

☐   Take into account the amount of attached fat when evaluating the price of a whole filet mignon. Untrimmed, that substance can account for about half the weight of the cut.

☐   Want an easy roast to cook? Buy a rib roast. You don't need an oven rack (the ribs perform that function) and you don't need to baste the meat (the fat layer performs this task).

☐   When buying a rib roast, tell the butcher that you want it cut from the larger end of the whole primal cut. That portion will have the most tender flesh and the highest lean-to-bone-and-fat ratio.

☐ A boned roast will be easier to carve, but it won't be as flavorful as a bone-in roast. Reason: Bones add flavor to the cooking meat.

☐ Tender cuts of meat (steaks and roasts from the rib, short loin, and sirloin primals) are usually best cooked with dry heat, such as roasting or broiling. Use moist heat, such as braising or stewing, for the relatively tougher cuts from the chuck, flank, and round primals.

☐ For broiling or barbecuing, select rib steaks that are at least 2 inches thick.

☐ The most tender chuck steak is the one that contains a cross section of a long, flat bone.

☐ Of the three round cuts (eye, top, and bottom), the eye round is the most expensive, yet is the toughest. Bard or marinate this meat, should you wish to roast it.

☐ The top round has the most tender meat of the three, while the bottom round generally offers the best all-around value because of its relatively low price.

☐ For the true and best London broil steak, buy the flank steak. (Most of the "London broil" meat sold in supermarkets is top round.)

☐ Buy fresh, not frozen, meat. The freezing and thawing processes cause the meat to lose some of its internal juices, which contribute flavor and nutrients and help keep the meat moist and tender as it cooks.

☐ When purchasing a steak or roast cut from the sirloin, short loin, rib, or chuck primal, look for ample marbling. The tiny embedded pockets of fat or marbling add flavor and keep the cooking meat moist.

Kitchen Hints

☐ A roast will have a crisper, more flavorful crust if you bring it to room temperature before cooking it.

☐ Though the technique is widely practiced, don't bard a tenderloin with bacon. Its flavor will overpower the tenderloin. Instead, use a strip of suet or unsalted fatback.

☐ The internal temperature of a roast will increase by about 5 degrees after you remove the roast from the oven. Therefore, pull the meat out of the oven a little before the desired internal temperature is reached.

☐ *See also* Broiling, Ground Beef, and Pan-Frying.

BEER

☐ Beer is a versatile yet often overlooked ingredient. You can substitute it for some or all of the water, wine, or stock in many of your recipes. You can steam clams or braise sausages in it. The possibilities are endless.

☐ Save your leftover beer for cooking; its flavor and acid are excellent for stews and bread dough. It doesn't matter that the beer is flat, because heat would have eliminated the effervescence anyway.

☐ For cooking, the full-flavored beers are generally preferable to their milder cousins.

☐ Don't cook with a run-of-the-mill beer or you'll end up with a run-of-the-mill dish.

☐ When making bread dough with beer, be sure to bring the brew to room temperature. Otherwise, the coldness of the liquid will slow down the growth of the yeast.

BEETS

☐ Don't throw away beet greens: Cook them as you would spinach.

☐ Cut the greens off the beets as soon as possible, because they draw out the nutrients and moisture.

☐ Never cut the stem closer than 1 inch from the bulb. Beets with miniscule stems bleed in the cooking water.

☐ Beets will also bleed if you peel them before they are cooked. Unless you are making a preparation like borscht soup, peel them after they are cooked.

☐ Scrub beets carefully. Should you rupture their thin skins, the beets may stain your hands or chopping board.

BERRIES

☐ If two boxes of berries are otherwise equal in desirability, weigh them on the greengrocer's scale. You may discover that one is a better value because it weighs more.

☐ Always examine the berries in the bottom of the box. They may be moldy or, if you see stains on the container, crushed.

☐ Should you find yourself with a surplus supply of berries, promptly convert them into a jam, jelly, or dessert sauce before they pass their prime.

BISCUITS

☐ Biscuits will become tough if you overmix the ingredients, as overhandling develops the gluten in the flour.

☐ Nor should you excessively cut the butter or fat into the flour. Unless you stop the task as soon as the mixture reaches the coarse crumb stage, your biscuits will be more dense than flaky.

BLACKBERRIES

☐ Choose fresh ripe blackberries which are full-shaped, stemless, glossy, and completely black.

☐ The first blackberries to reach the market in early summer are usually too tart for enjoyment. Wait a few weeks for better eating berries.

☐ A cooked blackberry preparation is usually best sieved because of the fruit's numerous seeds.

BLENDER

☐ If you've stored the blender in the attic when you purchased your new food processor, return it to your counter. A serious cook needs both appliances. While the food processor outperforms the blender for chopping chores, the blender does a better job emulsifying sauces and liquefying vegetables.

BLUEBERRIES

☐ Reject blueberries if their bloom has become dull and their configurations shriveled. They are past their prime.

☐ All the blueberries in a box should have a deep, rich hue; seeing a few green tinged ones does not auger well for the rest of them.

☐ If the box of blueberries you brought home from the store happens to have a few moldy or otherwise deteriorating fruits, discard them promptly before they spread their affliction.

☐ Never wash blueberries until you are ready to use them; surface moisture hastens spoilage.

☐ The best way to store blueberries is in a sealed plastic bag in the refrigerator. Eat them within a day or two, however, because they are quite perishable.

BOK CHOY

☐ A worthy bok choy has bright, unwilted leaves attached to crisp, unblemished stalks.

☐ Bok choy is at its best during the cool weather months.

☐ Bok choy cooks quickly. Stir-fry the leaves for only a minute or two. Several minutes is adequate to cook the cut up stalks.

☐ You can also eat bok choy raw. Try adding some to your next salad.

BRAINS

☐ The best tasting brains come from very young animals.

☐ Brains are extremely perishable; buy them only if they are plump, pinkish-white and free of off odors.

☐ Brains are also quite delicate. Handle them gingerly.

☐ Soak the brains in acidulated water in the refrigerator for an hour before you cook them. This makes it easier for you to remove the membrane casing, which could shrink and disfigure the brains. Soaking also helps draw out the blood, which turns brown, when cooked, spoiling the appearance of the flesh.

☐ If you are going to sauté the brains, blanch them first in acidulated water. This firms and whitens the flesh.

BRAISING

☐ For braising, select a pan only slightly larger than the food you are braising. By keeping the amount of air space within the pan to a reasonable minimum, you reduce the amount of steam inside the pan. If there is too much steam, the food will have the taste and texture of a steamed, rather than a braised, dish.

☐ Braising in the oven has two advantages over stove-top braising. The dish requires less pot watching and cooks more evenly because the heat envelops the entire vessel.

☐ Very lean cuts, such as bottom or eye round, will be noticeably more tender if you bard or lard them, or add ample fat to the braising liquid. Fattier cuts, such as pork shoulder, do not need these remedial measures.

☐ If you are browning meat that has been marinated, first pat it dry with paper towels. Otherwise, it will not brown properly.

BRAZIL NUTS

☐ The task of shelling the "toughest of nuts to crack" will be easier if you first roast the Brazil nuts in a preheated 375-de-

HOWARD HILLMAN

gree oven for 15 minutes. When cool, crack the shells lengthwise with a mallet or hammer.

BREAD

Marketplace Pointers

□ When buying packaged bread off the shelf, check both the date and the wrapper (it should be tightly sealed).

□ Whole wheat breads are generally more gastronomically exciting than white breads. They are also more nutritious.

□ Products labeled "wheat bread" are not necessarily made exclusively with whole wheat flours. The terms "whole wheat" and "100 percent whole wheat" on the label are your assurance that you are buying the genuine article.

□ Breads made with oils or fats will have a longer shelf life than those made strictly with flour and water, as are genuine French breads. Reason: The oil and fats hinder moisture loss. If there is too much of the incorporated oils and fats, however, the bread will be highly susceptible to rancidity.

Kitchen Hints

□ Though most people store bread in their refrigerator, that is not ideal. If you plan to consume the bread within one day, store it in a cool, dark spot. Wrap it snugly to minimize loss of moisture.

□ For a longer storage period, freeze the bread. (It is one of the few foods that can be frozen without undergoing an appreciable loss of texture.) Wrap the bread tightly, because bread readily absorbs freezer odors.

□ When using frozen bread, slice off what you'll need and return the unused portion to the freezer. The less it's exposed to air, the longer its storage life.

□ If your leftover fresh bread has dried out, but is otherwise still fresh, you can salvage it. Wrap the bread in a damp towel and refrigerate it for 6 hours. Unwrap and heat the bread in a preheated 300-degree oven for 5 to 10 minutes, depending on its thickness.

☐ Turn your leftover, slightly stale bread into bread crumbs. Pulverize the bread in a food processor and store the crumbs in a tightly sealed glass jar in the refrigerator.

BREAD BAKING

☐ Sweeteners, like sugar, honey, and molasses help to give breads flavor and a golden crust. They also serve as perservatives. On the negative side, they add empty calories and, if used in excess, can turn the bread into a dessert.

☐ Leftover potato cooking water provides nourishment for the yeast and flavor for your palate. Save it for your next bread baking project.

☐ You can give baking bread a hard crust by brushing it with water. If you want that crust to be golden brown, too, use beaten egg yolk instead of water.

☐ For a softer crust, brush baking breads with an oil or fat, such as butter.

☐ *See also* Bread Dough.

BREAD CRUMBS

☐ The best bread crumbs are homemade. The next time you have dried (slightly stale) bread, remove the crust and lightly pulverize the bread in your food processor with a steel blade. If the bread is not sufficiently dry, toast it in a preheated 200-degree oven for 10 to 15 minutes before you process it.

☐ When buying commercial bread crumbs, choose the ones that come in metal containers, because air can easily penetrate the paper-sided variety.

☐   Buy unseasoned bread crumbs. This allows you to season the bread crumbs in keeping with the dish and your whim.

☐   Out of bread crumbs? Try chopping an unsugared breakfast cereal, such as Shredded Wheat, in your blender or food processor.

BREAD DOUGH

☐   If you use milk instead of water, your bread will have a softer texture and a golden brown crust. On the other hand, water produces a chewier bread with a firmer crust.

☐   Some cooks make and freeze dough for future needs. Results are better if the dough is baked into bread before it is frozen.

☐   *See also* Bread Baking.

BREAKFAST CEREAL

☐   Don't buy breakfast cereals that come with raisins, other fruit, or nuts. Instead, purchase the cereal of your choice, and the dried or fresh fruit and nuts, separately; then mix them to taste. The fruit will be fresher and tastier and you will save money.

☐   Instead of using sugar to flavor your cereals, add a drop of vanilla extract to the milk.

☐   "Natural" on a label does not assure the consumer that a product is free, or virtually free, of sugar. Again, read the label.

☐   Most breakfast cereals are loaded with sugar—the contents of some reach 50 percent. Read the label (ingredients are listed in descending order of quantity). Be alert to sugars that are listed under the names of fructose, sucrose, maltose, and corn syrup.

☐   Buy whole grain cereals. They're more nutritious and contain more fiber.

□ Hot cereals become gummy if they are overcooked. Your clean up chores become harder, too.

□ The flavor and texture of instant hot cereals are so inferior to those of regular hot cereals that they are not worth the time they save you.

□ Your cooked breakfast cereals will be lighter in texture if you don't let the water stop boiling as you pour in the cereal. Do it gradually.

□ Once opened, a box of breakfast cereal will stay fresh much longer if you seal it within a plastic bag or transfer the contents to an airtight storage container.

BROCCOLI

Marketplace Pointers

□ Examine the bud clusters. They should be bright hued and tightly packed. If you see tiny flowers emerging from the buds, the vegetable is past its prime.

□ Broccoli stems should be slender and pliable. Woody stems indicate that the vegetable is overmature or has been stored too long.

□ Don't plan to serve broccoli during the hot weather months—good specimens are hard to find.

Kitchen Hints

□ For even cooking, remove the stalks, slice them into ½-inch-thick discs, and begin steaming or simmering them about 5 minutes before you add the flowerets.

□ Alternatively, marinate the uncooked disc-shaped stems overnight in an herb, olive oil, and vinegar mixture. Serve them as a raw snack.

□ A quick and nutrient-saving way to cook whole broccoli is

to stand the vegetable, stem and all, upright in 1 inch of rapidly boiling water. Cover the pot, reduce the heat slightly, and cook for 12 to 15 minutes, depending on size.

☐ Use a small, raw broccoli floweret as an edible garnish on a dinner plate or sandwich platter.

BROILING

☐ In order for the meat to sear properly, it should be at room temperature. Both the broiler and broiling pan should be preheated. It is also important to pat the meat dry before broiling.

☐ How close should you place the meat to the heat source of the broiler? Follow this guideline: The thinner the cut or the rarer you want the meat, the closer it should be to the heat source.

BROWN SUGAR

☐ Many cooks and diners erroneously think brown sugar is a health food. Laboratory tests prove that it is almost as nutritiously bankrupt as white sugar.

☐ Brown sugar will cake easily. Unlike white sugar, it should not be stored in a conventional sugar dispenser or bowl. Once you open the package, transfer the brown sugar to a jar with an airtight cover.

☐ *See also* Sugar.

BRUSSELS SPROUTS

Marketplace Pointers

☐ To guard against frequent deception in packaging, first remove the plastic wrapper of a container of brussels sprouts.

Examine a few samples from the bottom layers. Chances are that the unseen layers are not as worthy as the top layer.

☐ Avoid brussels sprouts whose leaves are dull-hued, loosely packed, wilted, or marred with worms or insect holes and nibbles.

☐ For the most tender brussels sprouts, buy the smallest you can find.

☐ Feast on brussels sprouts during their peak period—fall and winter.

Kitchen Hints

☐ Before cooking, remove any leaf that does not cling tightly to the vegetable. Those leaves tend to be tough.

☐ Brussels sprouts will cook quicker and more evenly if you score their stem ends with a deep "X" pattern.

☐ Steaming is the best cooking method for brussels sprouts. Normally, it only takes 10 minutes.

☐ When steaming brussels sprouts, add 1 teaspoon of mustard seeds to the water. The vegetable will be infused with a tangy mustard flavor.

☐ The best measure for doneness is the fork test. Try piercing the stem end of one of the brussels sprouts with the tines of a fork. The vegetable is done as soon as the tines can penetrate its heart without undue pressure. However, no resistance indicates overcooking.

☐ Another test for doneness is to monitor the hue of the outer leaves. The vegetable is done when the leaves turn a vivid green. If the vegetable is cooked for an appreciably longer period, it begins to turn a drab olive brown. It will also fill your kitchen with a malodorous scent.

BUTTER

Marketplace Pointers

☐ Buy unsalted butter. Salted butter can throw off your recipes because it is difficult to estimate how much salt the butter contains.

☐ Check the wrapper before you buy. The butter may have developed defects, such as rancidity, if its wrapper is torn, loose, or greasy.

☐ Sniff the butter. It should have a fresh, inviting aroma.

Kitchen Hints

☐ Whipped butter is better for sandwiches and pancakes, because it spreads easier than stick butter. On the other hand, stick butter is preferable for cooking, because its quantity can be measured more accurately.

☐ When sautéing, butter can scorch. A proven remedy is to substitute a quality cooking oil for part of the butter.

☐ Stored butter should be wrapped tightly because it can readily absorb the odors of its refrigerator mates.

☐ Need some butter for a recipe and there's none on hand? If you have heavy cream, you can make your own butter by whirling the cream and some ice cubes in your food processor, using a steel blade. This process coagulates the butterfat contained in the cream, creating a batch of white, unsalted butter.

☐ You can shorten the time it takes to cream cold butter if you first shred it with a potato peeler.

☐ Butter will also be easier to cream if you use a warm, but not hot, bowl.

☐ It will be easier to use a butter-curler if you occasionally dip its blade into warm (about 130 degrees) water. The butter should be refrigerator, not freezer-cold.

☐ Keep a supply of compound herb butter in your refrigerator for use as a quick topping for broiled steaks, baked potatoes, and other foods. To prepare it, blend a small quantity of finely chopped fresh herbs into softened butter. Chill before serving.

□   To keep your hands greaseless when rubbing a pan with butter, use a small discardable cellophane bag as a glove.

C

CABBAGE

☐ If a head is exceptionally white for its variety, it is over-mature and, therefore, not worth buying.

☐ Lift the cabbage. It should be heavy for its size.

☐ The head should be firm and compact for its variety. Cabbages with puffy heads have been stored too long.

☐ To tell whether a cabbage was harvested recently or stored in a warehouse for months, sniff it. New cabbages have a fresher and more inviting scent.

☐ Cabbage cooks quicker than most people realize: Shredded cabbage, for instance, cooks in a matter of minutes. If overcooked, the vegetable will fill your home with an unwelcome odor.

☐ To preserve the attractive hue of red cabbage, cook the vegetable with an acidy ingredient, such as tart apples or vinegar.

☐ To keep a cabbage wedge from breaking apart during cooking, first skewer it with one or two toothpicks.

☐ When making a stuffed cabbage entrée, it's critical to remove each whole cabbage leaf without tearing it. Chances of success improve if you first remove most of the core of the whole cabbage with a sharp knife. Then submerge the cabbage head in boiling water, turn off the heat and let the pot stand for several minutes before removing the cabbage. The now slightly softened cabbage leaves should come off with ease.

CAKES

☐ If a baking pan is too thin, the cake's bottom will likely scorch before its center is done.

☐ Occasionally a few unseen, oversized bubbles will form in the cake batter when you pour it into the pan. Rap the bottom of the pan a few times with your knuckles.

☐ Once you make the cake batter, don't let it sit or your cake may be unnecessarily dense. Start the baking process without delay.

☐ Near the end of the estimated baking time, stick a toothpick or thin skewer into the middle of the cake. If it comes out moist, the cake needs further baking.

☐ If your cake develops a dome when baked, try lowering the oven temperature by 10 degrees the next time. Naturally, you will have to extend the baking period slightly to compensate for the lower heat.

☐ If one side of your cake rises higher than the other side, chances are that one edge of the pan was placed too near an oven wall. It can also mean that your oven is not level. Compensate for this by revolving the pans 180 degrees halfway through the baking time.

☐ Before frosting a cake, brush away loose surface crumbs.

CALVES' LIVER

☐ Calves' liver is considerably more gastronomically rewarding than beef liver, because it is more delicate in aroma, taste, and texture.

☐ Occasionally, a store will market beef liver as calves' liver at the latter's higher price. You can spot the deception by examining the color. Calves' liver is pink-brown and beef liver is a deep reddish brown.

☐ Reject calves' liver if its surface is slimy or has a dull sheen.

☐ Liver is highly perishable. It should be cooked as soon as possible.

☐ Liver readily toughens and becomes bitter if overcooked, as would be the case if its interior changed from pink to brown.

☐ The best way to cook calves' liver is to slice it very thinly across the grain. Then sauté the pieces quickly over medium-high heat.

CANDLES

☐ Your candles will burn longer if you freeze them overnight. Remove them from the freezer just before you light them.

CAN OPENER

☐ If there is one area in your kitchen that likely plays host to pathogenic bacteria, it's the blade of your can opener. Use a pipe cleaner to scrub its hard-to-reach recesses.

CANS

☐ Never buy a dented or puffed up tin can. Botulism is one of the risks.

☐ For your health's sake, always wash the top of a tin can before you open it. It could have picked up insecticides, pathogenic microorganisms, insect droppings, or dust in the store.

Cantaloupes. *See* Melons.

CAPERS

☐ The capers sold in glass jars are past their prime if they have begun to acquire a brownish tint.

☐ Once you open a jar of capers, pour out the liquid and replace it with an undiluted plain quality vinegar. This doubles or triples the storage life of the capers.

☐ Replace your supply on a regular basis, because, even with the best of care, capers become mushy within a month or two after being opened.

CARDAMOM

☐ Your cardamom will be more flavorful if you purchase it in the pod rather than as shelled seeds. These seeds, however, are much more aromatic and tasty than preground cardamom.

☐ When buying cardamom in the pod, buy the green rather than the white pod variety. The latter is less flavorful because it has been bleached.

☐ You don't necessarily need to remove the seeds from the pod to flavor a soup or stew. Simply add the whole pod to the liquid and discard it before serving.

CARROTS

Marketplace Pointers

☐ Quality greengrocers leave the greens attached to let you judge the freshness of the carrots. If the tops are a vivid green and unwilted, the carrots are fresher than those displayed with greens detached.

☐ Ask the greengrocer to remove the green tops as soon as you buy the carrots, because they draw out the internal juices from the vegetable.

☐ If the carrots are sold without their green leaves, you can still tell their relative freshness by examining the stem end. If you see a green stalk stub, the carrots were recently harvested. If the stalk has been removed completely, then the carrot probably was stored for weeks or months in a warehouse.

☐ Avoid carrots that are unusually long or thick or which have cracked skins. Do the same if the stem end of the carrot is green-tinged (caused by excessive exposure to solar rays).

☐ Buy carrots that have a bright healthy glow, rather than a dull appearance.

☐ Limp carrots have deteriorated if they bend with light pressure. Don't buy them.

HOWARD HILLMAN

☐   Reject carrots with rootlets growing out of their sides. The rootlets indicate that the carrots are too old or that they have been stored too long.

Kitchen Hints

☐   It is possible to store carrots in a sealed plastic bag in the vegetable crisper for up to a week or so.

☐   Never store carrots with apples. Apples produce ethylene gas, which can make carrots bitter.

☐   Whether you peel a carrot depends largely on its age. Peel fully mature carrots. What you lose in nutrient value is offset by improvement in flavor. Baby and other young carrots need not be peeled.

☐   Sauté your carrots in butter or olive oil before adding them to a stew. The temperature caramelizes the sugars in the carrots, giving them a new flavor dimension.

☐   If you need only a few carrot shreds to add color to a salad, save clean up time by using your vegetable peeler, rather than your grater. Refrigerate the unused portion of the carrot in a sealed plastic bag.

CARVING

☐   Roast meat will be juicier if you wait 15 to 30 minutes before carving it. This allows the internal juices to settle and redistribute themselves after the meat comes out of the oven. Keep the roast warm during this period by placing it on a warm platter and covering the meat loosely with aluminum foil.

☐   Slice a cooked meat across the grain. This shortens the muscle fibers and, hence, makes the meat less chewy and more tender.

CAULIFLOWER

Marketplace Pointers

□   Peak season runs from fall to mid-winter.

□   The curds of white cauliflower, the most common variety, should be bleached and even-hued and void of discoloration and soft spots.

□   Whatever the size of the head, the curds should be firm and tightly packed.

□   The leaves should be vivid green, not browned or withered.

□   If you can't find a fresh cauliflower, don't substitute the frozen variety. The freezing and thawing processes rob the vegetable of one of its prized assets: crisp texture. Flavor and nutrients also fall victim to the freezing process.

Kitchen Hints

□   Fresh cauliflower is perishable. Store it in a sealed plastic bag in the vegetable crisper of your refrigerator and use it within a day or two.

□   The best all-around cooking method is steaming. Stir-frying also produces fine results. And, you don't necessarily have to cook cauliflower. It can be eaten raw as a crudité.

□   If you have a vegetable steamer basket, you can steam the cauliflower whole (though it helps to hollow out the stalk for the sake of even cooking). Top the cooked vegetable with a clinging and color-contrasting sauce, such as hollandaise, and a sprinkling of chopped parsley. Your whole cauliflower will make a striking presentation on the table. The leaves, incidentally, are edible.

□   Whatever the cooking method, don't overcook the cauliflower or the texture will become mushy, the food value will be diminished and the odor will be offensive.

HOWARD HILLMAN

☐ Keep the cauliflower bright white by adding 1 teaspoon of lemon juice or ½ teaspoon of vinegar to the cooking water. (Should your local water supply be particularly hard, even this measure won't work.)

☐ Because salt toughens cauliflower as it cooks, don't salt the vegetable until after it is cooked.

☐ Leftover cooked cauliflower makes a tempting crudité appetizer if you marinate it overnight in a vinaigrette sauce.

CAVIAR

☐ Only the roe from the sturgeon is true caviar. The relatively inexpensive bogus caviar found in supermarkets or other outlets is really white lumpfish roe that has been dyed black. It tastes atrocious.

☐ The most celebrated of the caviars sold in this country is the Beluga, but don't overlook the less expensive varieties, such as the Sevruga.

☐ Caviar, at its finest, consists of plump whole eggs. Pressed caviar can be a gastronomic bargain for thin walleted gourmets.

☐ Fresh caviar is better than the pasteurized kind. If a store sells fresh caviar, ask to sniff it before you purchase it. (The merchant should let you do this, considering the price he charges.) It should have a fresh taste and scent, void of any sourness or fishiness. The best grade is labeled *malossol*, the Russian term for "lightly salted."

☐ Fresh caviar must be kept at a temperature of just about 37 degrees. Do the same for pasteurized caviar, especially once it has been opened.

☐ To conserve flavor, serve the caviar in a dish (or in its original container), nestled in crushed ice.

☐ If you have purchased a quality caviar, don't eclipse its subtle flavor by serving it with sour cream, cream cheese, chopped onions, egg yolk, or lemon wedges. Instead accompany your precious caviar with crusty, thin, unseasoned toasted white bread or crackers. The two time-proven libation accompaniments are vodka or a dry champagne served ice cold.

CELERY

☐ Buy celery heads with crisp, unblemished stalks. The leaves should not be brown-tinged or withered.
☐ Store celery in a sealed plastic bag in the vegetable crisper. Use within the week, if not sooner.
☐ Farm dirt readily lodges itself between the stalks of the growing celery. Therefore, always scrub the stalks with a vegetable brush.
☐ Use the tougher outer stalks for cooking, such as braising. Reserve the more tender inner stalks for eating raw and the leaves for flavoring stocks and stews.
☐ To refresh a slightly limp celery stalk, stand it stem side down in a jar of ice water for an hour or two.

CHEESE

Marketplace Pointers

☐ Contrary to what some unscrupulous cheesemongers may tell you, no cheese should smell even slightly of ammonia. Neither should the surface rinds of Camembert and similar cheeses be blotched with an unsightly mold.
☐ A store that reeks of ammonia and moldy cheese is not the one you want to patronize. Quality cheesemongers have a good stock turnover and adequate ventilation.
☐ When possible, buy your cheese from a merchant who cuts pieces to order rather than displaying the precut cheeses. Your purchases will be fresher.
☐ Like wine, even the best of cheeses can vary markedly

from shipment to shipment. Ask to sample a cheese (good cheesemongers are happy to oblige) before buying it.

☐ If prepackaged, the covering should not be ripped or sticky.

☐ Whole soft cheese should be plump and resilient to finger pressure.

☐ Reject a brie if you see a thin white line running through its center or if the cheese has an exceptionally chalky white rind. Such cheese has not been aged properly.

☐ Quality brie is one of the few cheeses that will lose much of its admirable flavor if refrigerated. Therefore, buy no more than what you need for the day's consumption. Until you are ready to serve the brie, keep it tightly wrapped in plastic wrap and store it in a cool, dark, well-ventilated place.

☐ Blue cheese should have a creamy rather than a crumbly or dried out texture.

☐ Processed cheeses have longer storage lives and are easier to cook with than natural cheeses, but they lack the latter's depth of flavor and character.

☐ There are three basic quality levels of processed cheese. In descending order, they are "pasteurized processed cheese," "processed cheese food," and "processed cheese spread."

Kitchen Hints

☐ If you have a large piece of cheese and plan to serve it on more than one occasion, it will stay fresher if you cut off the portion you intend to consume and keep the remaining part in the refrigerator. Transferring the cheese back and forth between the refrigerator and dining table diminishes its flavor.

☐ With few exceptions, all cheeses should be kept tightly wrapped in plastic wrap or aluminum foil—and stored in the warmest part of your refrigerator. In addition, hard cheeses should be wrapped with a damp cloth before covering them with plastic wrap or foil.

☐ Cheese tastes best when served at room temperature. You can't fully appreciate the aroma and flavor of a refrigerator-cold cheese, because the chill numbs your palate and inhibits the release of the cheese's delicate aroma.

☐ Hard cheeses take longer to come to room temperature than soft ones of the same thickness.

☐ Soft cheeses don't freeze well. If you plan to use a hard cheese solely for cooking, you can freeze it satisfactorily, but only for a limited period of time.

☐ Don't throw away a cheese simply because it has surface mold. You can salvage the cheese by cutting out and discarding the moldy areas.

☐ Marinate a chunk of feta cheese in olive oil seasoned with rosemary. Serve with pita bread.

CHEESECAKE

☐ The surface of your homemade cheesecake is less likely to crack if you bake it in a humid oven. Set a water bath under the cheesecake pan and don't open the oven door until near the end of the baking time.

☐ Your cheesecake is also less likely to crack if you cool it in the turned-off oven. If you use this method, reduce the recipe's cooking time by a minute or two. Leave the oven door open during the first ten minutes of the cooling period.

CHEESE SAUCE

☐ To keep the cheese from becoming stringy, don't cook it too long or over high heat.

☐ A cheese will melt quicker in a sauce if you grate it or cut it into tiny pieces.

HOWARD HILLMAN

CHERRIES

☐ Resist the temptation to sample a cherry out of the green-grocer's bin unless you have a moist tissue to wash it. Cherries are usually coated with insecticides.

☐ Pick out the darkest hued cherries. They will be the most mature and ripe of the lot and, therefore, the sweetest and richest tasting.

☐ Each cherry should be plump and relatively firm without cuts or soft spots. The skin should have a healthy sheen.

☐ Sniff the cherries. A fermented odor indicates that they have been around too long.

☐ If you plan to store the cherries, always buy specimens with their stems still attached. For immediate consumption, a stemless, but otherwise perfect, cherry offers you a value since cherries are sold by weight.

☐ If the cherry has been harvested recently, the stem will be flexible, not stiff.

☐ Store cherries in a sealed plastic bag in the refrigerator.

☐ Wash the cherries just before consumption. The washing period should be short lest they absorb water.

CHESTNUTS

☐ Fresh chestnuts become rancid quickly. If you have a surplus supply, freeze them in their shells in a plastic bag for up to one month. Then thaw, peel, and purée them.

☐ Roasting chestnuts in the fireplace can be hazardous unless you create an escape for the built-up steam. Do this by cutting an "X" pattern through the flat side of the shell. These incisions also make peeling easier.

CHICKEN

Marketplace Pointers

☐ Choose a mature chicken for roasting, braising, or stewing. Reason: It is more flavorful and has more meat per pound of dressed weight than a young one.

☐ For broiling or frying, however, you should select a young chicken, one that is relatively small for its variety. Unlike the flesh of a mature chicken, that of a young one is tender enough to be cooked quickly with a very high heat.

☐ Buy fresh, not frozen, chicken. The meat of a frozen bird will be tougher because, when it thaws, it will lose a fair portion of its internal juices.

☐ You know the chicken has been frozen (or partially frozen) and then thawed, if you see liquid in the container. That liquid has leeched out of the bird.

☐ The criterion "the deeper hue the skin, the better the chicken" is meaningless in today's marketplace, because many producers cunningly feed their chickens marigold petals so they attain that skin color. The floral pigmentation literally dyes the skin of the bird yellow.

☐ Sniffing the chicken is the surest test for freshness. Don't buy it if you detect even a slight off odor.

☐ Chicken skin should be moist, smooth, and free of abrasions and discoloration.

☐ When buying a whole chicken, look for a symmetrical structure and firm, plump flesh.

☐ If you buy the chicken with its head still attached (as Europeans do), inspect the cockscomb. It should be a bright, vivid red.

☐ When buying chicken parts, examine the color of the exposed flesh. It should have a fresh blush and not be dull or grayish. Also ascertain whether there is ample fat below the skin, a sign of a well-fed bird.

☐ Chicken legs should be squat for their size.

HOWARD HILLMAN

□ You can tell the relative age of a chicken by bending the tip of the breastbone. The more flexible this bone, the younger the chicken.

□ If you cook a lot of chicken, you can save a considerable sum over the course of a year if you buy the chickens whole and cut them up yourself. (Butchers, remember, are well-paid tradespersons.)

Kitchen Hints

□ If the chicken you buy is tightly wrapped in plastic wrap and you don't plan to cook the chicken within the next few hours, remove and discard that covering. Otherwise, no air can circulate inside the package and, as a consequence, the surface of the chicken will remain moist. That moisture provides a splendid medium for the proliferation of bacteria. Before refrigerating, rewrap the chicken loosely in butcher or wax paper.

□ Don't thaw a chicken at room temperature, because bacteria will multiply quickly. Instead, thaw the bird in the refrigerator. (Allow at least several hours for parts and a full day for a whole chicken.) As a bonus, a frozen chicken will lose less of its internal juices with the slow-thaw method.

□ Bring refrigerated chicken to or near to room temperature before you start to cook it. Allow 30 to 40 minutes for an average-sized whole chicken and 15 to 20 minutes for chicken parts.

□ When you are cooking a whole chicken leg, be sure to make an incision halfway through the joint connecting the thigh and drumstick so that the heat can better penetrate that area. Otherwise, one of two possibilities will occur: 1. the meat surrounding the joint will be undercooked by the time the rest of the leg is cooked; or 2. the rest of the leg will be overcooked by the time the meat surrounding the joint is cooked.

□ For the same reason, you should cut halfway through the skin at the large joint of a chicken wing.

☐ Though boneless chicken breasts are easier to cook, the bone-in breasts have their advantages. The bones reduce shrinkage, contribute flavor, and help thicken sauces.

☐ Your boneless chicken breasts will shrink less when cooked if you cut out the white tendon that runs lengthwise through the meat.

☐ A whole chicken should be trussed before roasting even if you don't stuff it. Besides keeping the stuffing (if any) inside the cavity, trussing helps to assure even cooking and maintains body shape.

☐ The breast meat of a whole chicken will be done sooner than the leg meat unless you cover it for part of the roasting period. The popular method of using aluminum foil to cover the breast is an unsound tactic, because the foil traps moisture which steams the breast meat, producing a mushy texture. A better approach is to use a double layer of cheesecloth, which has been dipped in melted butter.

☐ If you want a crisp skin, don't salt the exterior of the bird until near the completion of the cooking time. Salt draws out the juices of the chicken, thereby keeping the skin moist, which hinders browning.

☐ The older or larger the chicken, the lower the temperature and the longer the roasting period should be. The basic time formula for room-temperature chicken is 20 minutes plus 15 to 20 minutes per pound. The proper oven temperature varies from 325 degrees for a large capon to 400 degrees for a small Rock Cornish hen.

☐ To test a whole roasted chicken for doneness, insert a meat thermometer into the thickest area of the thigh. For an accurate reading, don't let the tip of the thermometer touch a bone. The chicken is cooked to a medium-to-well-done state when the indicator reaches 165 degrees. For a well-done chicken, add 15 degrees.

☐ The roasted chicken will be easier to carve and will lose less of its internal juices if you delay the carving. Place it on a warm platter and cover the bird loosely with aluminum foil. Let a small chicken rest for 10 minutes and a larger one for 20 minutes.

☐ When sautéing or broiling, don't add the pepper until near the end of the cooking period because high heat scorches the spice, making it bitter. Salt should be reserved for the end, too, because it draws moisture to the surface of the broiling or sautéing food, and, as a result, impedes browning.

☐ A chicken piece will stick less to the pan if you begin sautéing it skin side down. Bone-in chicken breasts are the exception. Start them bone side down.

☐ The problem of sticking will also be minimized if the chicken has been brought to room temperature and has been patted dry with paper toweling. Also, be sure the fat or oil is sufficiently hot.

CHICKEN SOUP DUMPLINGS

☐ Mix chopped leftover chicken with a flour, egg, and water dumpling batter. Cook and serve the combination with your next chicken soup.

CHILI PEPPERS

☐ Chili enthusiasts, beware: In an attempt to broaden the market, agro-scientists are developing chilies with less fire. This means that you have to buy more of these newfangled chilies to achieve the same degree of hotness. Save money by buying your chilies from a greengrocer who still sells the "old-fashioned" strains.

☐ Buy plump, unshriveled chili peppers with bright-hued skins. Reject any with soft spots, cuts, or bruises.

☐ The less twisted the chili pepper, the easier it will be to prepare.

☐ Store chili peppers in sealed plastic bags in the vegetable crisper. If you plan to keep the chilies for more than a couple of days, pierce the bags.

☐   If you want to reduce the hotness of chili peppers, remove the seeds and membranes. To further diminish their hotness, parboil them for several minutes.

☐   Certain oils in the chili pepper can burn your skin and, especially, your eyes. Make it a habit to wash your knife and chopping block as well as your hands promptly after cutting chili peppers.

☐   Under no circumstances should you rub your eyes before you've completed this cleansing chore. If you inadvertently do, quickly wash your fingers and flush out the afflicted eye(s) with cool water.

CHILI POWDER

☐   To increase the hotness of commercial chili powder, add cayenne pepper.

☐   Even better, blend your own chili powder mixture. Combine and grind these herbs and spices: oregano, cumin, cayenne pepper, cloves, and allspice. Add finely minced fresh garlic just before you use the powder.

CHILI SAUCE

☐   If the hue of your Tabasco or other bottled chili sauce has changed from red to brown, replace it because the product has lost most of its fresh fruity flavor.

CHIVES

☐   Whether the chives are sold potted or as freshly cut stems, they should be bright green, unwilted, and free of sliminess. There should be no hint of a sour scent.

☐   Given a choice, buy potted chives. They will be fresher than the cut variety and the supply will last you a long time. Simply use a pair of scissors to cut off the quantity you need.

HOWARD HILLMAN

☐ When you harvest potted chives, snip off a few whole blades, rather than lopping off the tops of all the blades. If you don't, the tips of the remaining stalks will brown.

☐ The dried chopped chives available in jars and tins have lost too much of their original characteristic aroma and flavor to be worth their price.

☐ The frozen chopped chives sold in small plastic tubs usually prove to be wasteful. Unless you use the chives on a daily basis, they will likely become frosty and clumpy long before you use up the supply. If you inadvertently return the tub to the refrigerator rather than the freezer, the chives can not be refrozen effectively.

☐ Freshly cut whole chives will keep for several days if you wrap them in damp paper towels, seal them in a plastic bag, and store the package in the vegetable crisper. Or you can place them root end down in a partially filled jar of water and cover the stalks with a plastic bag fastened to the jar with a rubber band; then store in the refrigerator.

☐ Chives are one of the most delicately flavored members of the onion family and can quickly lose their subtleties if they are cooked for more than a brief period. It is best to sprinkle them on a dish after it is cooked, thereby preserving their flavor and appeal as a garnish.

☐ Even in the refrigerator, chopped chives deteriorate quickly and develop a harsh bitter-sour taste. Therefore, don't prepare a mixture like cream cheese and chives too far in advance.

☐ Use chive stalks to tie carrots into eye-catching individual serving bundles. To make the chives more pliable, blanch them in boiling water for 15 seconds.

CHOCOLATE

Marketplace Pointers

☐ If possible, examine the surface of the chocolate when you buy it: A sheen suggests freshness; an off-white bloom indicates improper or prolonged storage.

☐ Your cookies and other sweets will taste considerably better if you buy genuine chocolate chips rather than chocolate-flavored chips. The latter product is made with hydrogenated vegetable oil instead of cocoa fat.

☐ Don't buy liquid chocolate. Though it has the advantage of being premelted, it is made with vegetable oil instead of cocoa butter. Taste and texture suffer.

Kitchen Hints

☐ Don't refrigerate chocolate; the change in temperature will cause the cocoa butter to rise to the surface of the chocolate, creating an off-white bloom.

☐ To store chocolate, wrap it tightly in plastic wrap. Keep it in a cool, dry, dark, well-ventilated place.

☐ Out of bitter chocolate? Substitute 3 tablespoons of cocoa powder plus 1 tablespoon of unsalted butter for each ounce or square of bitter chocolate.

☐ Chocolate should always be melted slowly over low, indirect heat. A double boiler fits the bill. You can also use a pan set on a flametamer over low heat.

☐ Moisture can stiffen melting chocolate. Therefore, be sure the steam from the lower pot of a double broiler doesn't curl over the rim of the upper pot.

☐ Melting a small quantity of chocolate in a pan is wasteful. Instead, place it in a small bowl set inside a skillet containing a shallow layer of gently simmering water.

CHOPPING BOARD

☐ Your board will last longer if you follow these steps before using it for the first time. Scour it with hot soapy water, thoroughly rinse it, and let it dry for about 30 minutes. Then, give it a generous coating of odorless mineral or vegetable oil. Repeat this step every hour until the board stops absorbing the oil. Let it stand overnight. The next morning, wipe off the excess oil and you are ready to start chopping.

CINNAMON

☐ Much of the cinnamon sold in America comes from the bark of the cassia rather than from the true cinnamon tree. The imposter is more bitter and is recognizable by its lighter hue.
☐ Stick cinnamon is more aromatic and has a longer storage life than preground cinnamon.
☐ Add stick cinnamon to stews and remove it prior to serving.

CLAMS

Marketplace Pointers

☐ For the most tender and delicately flavored clams, select those that are small for their variety.
☐ The peak season for most clam species is fall through spring.
☐ Give the clam shell a light tap. If a hard-shell clam does not close or if the neck of a soft-shell clam does not contract, the clam is dead or dying.
☐ Leave clams with broken shells in the bin; they could be a health hazard. Do the same if a clam feels heavy or light for its size. The heavy one may be filled with sand; the light one may be long dead.
☐ Select even-sized clams to assure even cooking.

Kitchen Hints

☐ Clams will expel the sand inside their shells if you store them overnight in a container of cool water in the refrigerator or in a cool spot. They will also rid themselves of some of their previously digested food if you sprinkle the water with a fine-textured cornmeal, which they will eat.

☐ Throw away any clams that float. They are filled with gas that develops when matter decays.

☐ If you are a novice clam opener, you can make your chore easier by putting the bivalves in the freezer for 5 to 15 minutes before you begin to open them. A longer period, however, will ruin the flavor and texture of the flesh.

☐ You can diminish the chances of cutting yourself while opening a clam if you wear an ordinary work glove on the hand that holds the mollusk.

☐ If a cooked clam refuses to open, don't try to pry its shells apart. The mollusk is likely inedible.

☐ Simmer, never boil, a clam preparation. Otherwise, the flesh shrivels and becomes leathery.

☐ A steamed or simmered clam is done when the shell opens. Further cooking will toughen the delicate flesh.

CLAY COOKING POTS

☐ Clay cooking pots are less likely to crack if you soak them in hot water for at least 15 minutes before you place them in the oven or over a flame. In the latter case, take the added precaution of using a flametamer.

CLOVES

☐ When in doubt about the freshness of dried whole cloves, crush the head of a sample. The released scent of the clove should be pronounced. Its texture should not be unduly brittle.

☐ Use cloves sparingly; they are among the strongest flavored spices.

COCONUTS

☐ Because of its high oil content, coconut flesh becomes rancid quickly when it is exposed to the air. Therefore, when buying pregrated coconut, choose the product that comes in a tin can rather than in a plastic pouch.

☐ To judge a whole coconut, first lift it. It should feel heavy for its size.

☐ Shake the coconut next to your ear. If it's fresh, you'll hear and feel its internal liquid sloshing.

☐ Examine the three "eyes" in the whole coconut. They should be dry and without any trace of mold.

☐ Reject whole coconuts with cracks. Bacteria can enter through these fissures and spoil the coconut flesh.

☐ To open a coconut, first pierce two of its eyes with a sturdy screwdriver (pour out and reserve the liquid for possible use in another preparation). Bake the coconut in a 325-degree oven for 20 minutes. If the heat has not ruptured the shell, wrap the coconut in a towel and give it a few hearty blows with a mallet or other heavy instrument.

COFFEE

Marketplace Pointers

☐ There is no comparison between the goodness of coffee made from freshly ground beans and that from preground canned coffee. The latter is less aromatic and has a harsher, less pleasing flavor.

☐ You are apt to end up with a lot of stale and broken coffee beans if you buy the beans out of a nearly empty burlap bag. Select beans from a full or nearly full sack—and from a store that has a fast turnover.

☐ Decaffeinated beans, if freshly ground and of high quality, can make a tempting cup of coffee. Unfortunately, most of the decaffeinated coffees on the market leave much to be desired.

☐ Freeze-dried coffee tastes better than regular instant coffee. Neither, however, can please true coffee lovers.

☐ If you enjoy the flavored coffees on the market, try flavoring your own. For instance, add a pinch of cardamom or nutmeg to the ground coffee before you brew it.

Kitchen Hints

☐ Coffee beans stay fresh longer if you store them in the freezer rather than in the refrigerator or at room temperature.

☐ Once ground, coffee loses its aromatics quickly. Grind only the quantity you need for immediate consumption. Should you wish to prepare a larger amount for the sake of convenience, prepare no more than what you will need for the next day or two—and store that supply in an airtight container in the refrigerator.

☐ A large economy-sized can of coffee is no bargain if you don't consume it within a week or two after you open the lid. For optimum freshness, the can also must be kept tightly closed and refrigerated.

COFFEE-MAKING EQUIPMENT

☐ Unless you brush the coffee particles out of your grinder after each use, these bits and pieces may become rancid and bitter, flavoring the next batch of beans you grind.

☐ You can brew a great cup of coffee with the drip method, but never with a percolator. Reason: A percolator boils coffee and consequently makes it bitter.

☐ Coffee also becomes bitter if it is kept on a warmer for more than 10 minutes or so.

☐ If you want to reheat leftover coffee, the best method is to bring it to a temperature of approximately 170 degrees in a microwave oven.

COLD DISHES

☐ If you are testing a dish for seasoning that is currently hot but will be served cold, add more seasoning than your taste-buds dictate. The colder the food, the less pronounced its aroma and taste will be.

COLLARD GREENS

☐ Collard greens need not be tough and fibrous. Buy young specimens that don't have seed stems.

☐ The leaves should be a vivid dark green, not withered, yellow-tinged, or riddled with bug holes.

☐ Collard greens normally require several washings in luke-warm water to rid them of clinging dirt.

☐ Unless you buy very young collard greens, steaming won't tenderize the leaves. Simmer them, instead.

☐ Because collard greens have a strong flavor, they partner poorly with delicately flavored foods, such as broiled fillet of sole. Serve them with hearty fare, such as a pot roast.

COMMERCIAL MEAT TENDERIZERS

☐ Commercial meat tenderizers do not tenderize the meat uniformly. When cooked, the flesh near the surface tends to be mushy. The best meat tenderizer is still the traditional mari-nade, a mixture of vinegar (or other acidic liquid), oil, and seasonings, such as herbs and spices.

CONDIMENTS

☐ Condiments, such as mustard and ketchup, and spreads, such as peanut butter, retain their aromatics and flavors longer if you refrigerate them once they are opened.

COOKIES

☐ To help prevent your cookies from burning on the bottom, use a heavy gauged steel baking sheet rather than the common thin aluminum ones.

☐ If your cookie dough is made with an ample quantity of butter or shortening, you don't need to grease the baking sheet.

☐ Let a baking sheet cool before you add a new batch of cookie dough lest the heat causes the dough to spread. Moreover, the extra heat may cause the bottom of the cookies to scorch before the interiors are properly baked.

☐ Your cookies will less likely fall apart if you let them cool completely before transferring them to the cookie jar.

☐ Use the crumbs in the bottom of a cookie jar or box as a topping to sprinkle on ice cream and other desserts.

CORN

Marketplace Pointers

☐ Buy for immediate consumption, because the flavor of corn deteriorates noticeably within days after it has been harvested. Some corn connoisseurs define that period in hours, if not minutes.

☐ Look for vivid green husks that snugly encase the kernels. These husks should not be yellowed, wilted, moist, or dry.

☐ The exposed silk should visually and tactilely remind you of silk. If it has started to brown and dry out, the corn has been around too long.

HOWARD HILLMAN

☐ Examine the stem end. The cut surface should be relatively soft and moist. A woody texture indicates prolonged or improper storage.

☐ Sniff the corn. It should smell garden fresh.

☐ Peel back part of the husk to inspect at least one third of the kernels. The rows should be parallel, not crooked or crowded. The area near the tip of the cob should not have missing or stunted kernels. Each kernel should be plump and—when pressed with your finger—springy. If you cut into one of them, it should exude a milky, as opposed to a watery, liquid.

☐ Don't buy prehusked corn, if possible. By removing the natural protective wrapping, the greengrocer has accelerated the corn's deterioration.

☐ Frozen and canned corn has lost too much of its flavor, texture, and nutrients to be taken seriously by any true lover of fresh vegetables.

Kitchen Hints

☐ If you must store corn, seal in a plastic bag and refrigerate it.

☐ The quickest way to remove silk that clings to a freshly shucked ear of corn is to rub the exposed kernels with a slightly moistened paper towel or under cool running water.

☐ The fresher the corn, the quicker it cooks. Cook the corn in a generous quantity of rapidly boiling water for about 3 minutes if it was recently picked. Double that period if it is storebought but still reasonably fresh. Over-the-hill corn takes 10 minutes, but it isn't worth eating in the first place.

☐ Cover the cooking pot. This traps the steam which will cook any corn protruding out of the boiling water.

☐ Corn kernels toughen if you add salt to the boiling water at the beginning of the cooking process. Add the salt during the last 30 seconds, or let each diner season according to his taste.

☐ To barbecue shucked corn, coat it with butter and herbs, wrap it tightly in aluminum foil, and bury the package in the hot coals. It will be done in 10 to 15 minutes, depending on thickness and freshness. (The fresher the corn, the shorter the required cooking time.)

CORN BREAD

☐   If your baking pan (or oven) is very hot before you add the batter, your corn bread will acquire a desirable thick crust.

CORNMEAL

☐   Your corn bread will be more flavorful and will have a better texture if you use cornmeal that has been water- or stone-ground rather than ground with steel rollers. The water-ground is also more nutritious because it still contains the germ (embryo).
☐   Store the roller-ground cornmeal in an airtight container in a cool, dark place. Water-ground cornmeal needs to be refrigerated to prevent rancidity.

CRABS AND CRABMEAT

☐   There are three basic grades of crabmeat: lump (large chunk); backfin (smaller chunks); and flake (bits and pieces). If you are making a preparation like a soufflé, save money by buying the flake grade. For salads, though, the lump grade is worth its premium price.
☐   When buying a whole uncooked crab, make sure it's alive and snapping. Once dead, bacteria spreads quickly thoughout the flesh—and there's no way for you to know how long ago the creature died.
☐   Before you buy a whole cooked crab, sniff it for any off odors.
☐   Crabs are their sweetest and most tender when young.

HOWARD HILLMAN

Choose crab specimens that are relatively small for their variety.

☐ Frozen and canned crabmeat tend to be mushy and discolored and emit some off odors. Save your money for fresh crabmeat.

☐ If you like the roe, here's how to spot the female. Turn the crab over and examine the apron, the rear portion of the crustacean's lower carapace. For most of the available edible crab species, the female's carapace is broader and larger than the male's. If you buy an uncooked blue crab, you can also look at the claws: Those belonging to a female will be red tipped.

☐ Soak the crabs in warm water (about 140 degrees) for at least 15 minutes. This procedure helps cleanse the crab's surface of slime. It also slows down its metabolism, and, thus, will put up less of a fighting protest when you plunge it into the boiling water.

CRACKER SPREAD

☐ Blend leftover blue cheese with half its volume of butter and a smidgen of apple brandy. Cover and refrigerate for up to a couple of weeks. Serve as a spread for crackers or as a topping for baked potatoes.

CREAM

☐ Good cooks find ultrapasteurized cream unsatisfactory, though it can be stored longer than regular cream. It doesn't whip as well and it has a slightly baked flavor.

☐ Before you buy one of those non-dairy "whipped cream" aerosols, read the label. You may need a degree in chemistry to decode it.

☐ Cream whips best if it and the bowl and beater are refrigerator cold.

KITCHEN SECRETS

☐   When whipping cream, add the sugar just before the foam reaches its full volume. If added earlier, expansion will be impeded. If added later, the mixture will be overwhipped by the time the sugar is thoroughly incorporated into the cream.

☐   If you use cream in your coffee, it must be very fresh. Otherwise, it will curdle.

CREAM SOUPS

☐   Your cream soups may curdle if you add the cream before the very end of the cooking period. The temperature of the soup should not be higher than 180 degrees (a slow simmer).

CRÈME FRAÎCHE

☐   If crème fraîche is unavailable, you can make a reasonable facsimile by adding 1 teaspoon of buttermilk to 1 cup of heavy cream. Let the mixture stand at room temperature for about 6 hours, or until thickened. Then use or refrigerate. It is perfect as a topping on fresh fruit, such as raspberries.

CRÊPES

☐   Overbeating the batter develops the gluten in the flour and thereby guarantees a leaden crêpe. For a light and airy crêpe, stop the mixing just before the batter becomes smooth.

☐   The pan must be hot before you add the batter. Once you add it, swirl the pan promptly to coat its entire bottom before the batter firms.

☐   For best results, use the minimum amount of batter necessary to coat the pan's bottom. Usually that's about 1 liquid ounce of batter per standard-sized crêpe pan.

CRUDITÉS

☐ To give vegetables, such as celery and carrots, added crispness for use as a crudité, soak them in ice water in the refrigerator for at least an hour.

CUCUMBERS

☐ The elongated, so-called "gourmet" cucumbers on the market are generally the best bet. They cost more, but you get better flavor and virtually no waste. Because they are sealed in plastic wrap, rather than being waxed, you don't have to peel them.

☐ Whatever the variety of cucumber, select the smallest specimens in any given bin, even if all the cucumbers are priced equally. The larger ones are more mature and, therefore, are more bitter. They also have tougher skins and more seeds.

☐ The skin of the cucumber should be solid green without blemishes, white streaks, or soft spots.

☐ Waxed cucumbers are not desirable because there are some preparations that benefit by the color and texture of the skins. Even though the wax is edible, you must (or at least should) peel a wax cucumber. Reason: The wax coating can trap insecticides and other unwanted substances between it and the skin.

☐ Unbeknownst to many cooks, cucumbers can be braised, steamed, or stir-fried with marvelous results. For instance, in combination with the cucumbers, try diced sweet red peppers to add color, flavor, and texture contrast. Select an herb, such as dill or basil for seasoning.

CURRY POWDER

☐ Commercial curry blends are seldom worth buying, because they are usually overstretched with the relatively inexpensive turmeric spice which becomes bitter when subjected to high heat. You're better off blending your own curry by mixing ground spices, such as cumin, cardamom, coriander seeds, cayenne pepper, mace, nutmeg, cinnamon, and saffron. If you decide to add turmeric, do it sparingly.

☐   To make the distinctive flavor of the key individual spices in a dried curry mixture stand out in the finished dish, roast the whole dry spices for 20 minutes in a preheated 250-degree oven before grinding them.

CUSTARDS

☐   To prevent your custard from weeping, don't bake it at too high a temperature or for too long. Also, cook just enough for one meal as the cold temperature of a refrigerator will cause most custards to weep.

☐   Your custard will not set properly if the liquid in the water bath boils. Should you see the water begin to boil, promptly lower its temperature by adding ¼ cup of cold water. Then, lower the oven temperature.

D

DAIKONS

□ Though daikons are naturally large, you should buy the smallest specimens for the species. The root should feel firm and heavy for its size. The skin should be uncracked and free of blemishes.

□ Store daikons in a sealed plastic bag in the vegetable crisper.

DANDELION GREENS

□ Dandelion greens are at their best in the springtime.

□ Those bothersome dandelions that proliferate on your lawn, are edible if they grow in an area free of dogs, foot traffic, and lawn chemicals. They should be harvested before they flower.

□ Choose small dandelion greens—they are more tender and delicately flavored than the mature ones.

□ Reject any dandelion greens that show evidence of wilting or browning or insect damage.

□ If the dandelion greens are a bit too tough to eat raw in a salad, try braising them in butter or olive oil with minced scallions, white wine vinegar, fresh parsley, and salt and pepper.

DATES

□ Should the dates in a package stick tightly together, warm them in a preheated 300-degree oven for several or more minutes. Separate and let stand at room temperature for 15 minutes before serving.

☐ Freshly harvested dates should be plump. Even dried ones should be reasonably plump, not excessively shriveled or dried out.

☐ Reject dates that have sticky skins. Dates covered with tiny sugar crystals have seen better days. A sour scent is also a negative sign.

☐ Dates should not be finely minced, lest you create a sticky paste.

☐ Soak dried dates in Madeira wine and serve as a light dessert.

DEEP-FRYING

☐ Most foods should be breaded or coated with a batter before being deep-fried. Otherwise, some of the moisture in the food will come in contact with the oil, causing a messy and hazardous splatter.

☐ Potatoes need not be breaded or batter-coated, because the pores of their exposed flesh are sealed quickly by the hot oil.

☐ Be diligent about applying batter or crumb coating to the food. If you leave uncoated patches, the food will absorb the oil, calories and all.

☐ Breaded and batter-coated food should be allowed to dry for 30 minutes at room temperature prior to submerging it in the hot cooking oil. This time period allows some of the water in the batter to evaporate, thus helping to minimize the splatter created when the water comes in contact with the hot oil. A second major advantage is that the batter will cling better to the food.

☐ The ideal deep-frying temperature for most foods is in the 365- to 375-degree range.

☐ Some cookbooks misadvise: "Don't start deep-frying until a haze forms over the oil." As that haze is smoke, the oil has reached the smoking point and is thereby rapidly decomposing.

HOWARD HILLMAN

☐ If you don't have a deep-fat thermometer, place a 1-inch cube of crustless white bread into the oil. The oil temperature is approximately 375 degrees if it takes 40 seconds for the bread to develop a uniform brown surface.

☐ Olive oil is not recommended for deep-frying because it has too low a smoking point (about 375 degrees).

☐ The smoking point of sesame oil is sufficiently high (roughly 420 degrees) for effective deep-frying, but its flavor is too assertive for most foods and tastes. However, a small amount can be used to flavor another oil, for the sake of flavor enrichment.

☐ Safflower oil is the best of the commonly available cooking oils for deep-frying. Peanut oil is the runner-up.

☐ Don't be miserly with the quantity of oil you use. Neither should you add too much food to the oil at one time, nor crowd the pan. Any of these approaches will lower the temperature of the oil and, thereby, make the food greasy.

☐ Use a pan deep enough to hold the oil with several inches of space to spare. When you add the food, the oil and its bubbles will rise.

☐ Strain an oil through a funnel lined with cheesecloth before storing it for reuse. This will remove burnt food and other particles that will turn the oil rancid as well as darken it and give it an off flavor.

☐ If you deep-fry fish, do not reuse the oil to cook other types of food. Otherwise, the food may acquire a fishy odor and taste.

☐ If you can't serve your crumb- or batter-coated deep-fried foods immediately, keep them warm in a preheated 300-degree oven. Reminder: Their coatings will become soggy and greasy if you hold them in this environment for more than 15 minutes.

DEFROSTING

☐ When the frost builds up in a freezer and reaches ½ inch thick, the electricity expense becomes twice that of a defrosted unit. Postponing the task is expensive in this day of high energy bills.

DIETING

☐ When reading a label, know the federally defined distinction between the phrases "low calorie" and "reduced calories." The first defines a product with 40 or fewer calories per standard serving; "reduced calories" means the product has at least one-third fewer calories than regular brands.

☐ The term "light" on a food label has no official meaning. The product could be low calorie or not.

☐ Products labeled "no sugar added" may be just as fattening as those with sugar. Sometimes the food processing company substitutes high-calorie sweeteners, such as fructose, dextrose, honey, or corn syrup, for the sucrose sugar. Read the list of ingredients on the label.

☐ The light meat of chicken or turkey has fewer calories than the dark meat.

☐ Some dieters choose to cook with white rather than red wine in the mistaken belief that it is less fattening. Both have approximately the same number of calories (25 per ounce if dry and 40 if sweet).

☐ "Bananas are fattening" is a myth. The average-sized banana has only about 85 calories.

☐ You can reduce the amount of cream and butter needed to thicken a sauce if you add a vegetable pureé prepared in your blender or food processor.

☐ Yogurt can be used as a relatively low calorie, low cholesterol substitute for cream in cream soups. The flavor and texture will be different, but the soup will be good on its own merits.

☐ The "Silverware Diet" is one of the most effective yet overlooked weight-reducing techniques. Cut the food into smaller morsels and set your fork down between bites.

DINNER PARTIES

☐ In the hectic last-minute rush to bring the various dishes to the dining table, it's not uncommon for a host or hostess to forget to serve an item, such as breadsticks or a relish. Prepare a checklist menu ahead of time and keep it handy.

☐ Buy a loose-leaf notebook or a set of index cards to record information on what you served a particular guest and what he or she liked and disliked. This helps you plan future menus without fear of repeating dishes unnecessarily.

☐ Short of kitchen counter space when preparing a large number of preparations? Set up your ironing board.

DISH SOAKING

☐ Egg and flour residue is easier to remove from a plate or utensil soaked in lukewarm water. Soaking the ware in hot water would be counterproductive, because high temperatures set the protein in egg yolks and makes flour gummy. Cold water soaking is preferable to the hot method but not as effective as the lukewarm one.

DOUGHNUTS

☐ For tender homemade doughnuts, use cake flour. All-purpose flour and especially bread flour produce heavy, leaden doughnuts.

DRIED FRUITS

☐ Prunes, raisins, and other dried fruits that have slightly hardened during storage can be rescued by soaking them in a little hot water in a covered bowl at room temperatures for 30 minutes. Drain, pat dry, and serve.

☐   Dried fruits will stick less to a knife when you chop them if you dip the blade into a pot of boiling water every 15 seconds.

☐   Generally, dried fruits, such as apricots and apples, are best soaked in cold water for about 30 minutes before you cook them.

DUCK

☐   Shop for a duck that is small for its variety and that has a fleshy, expansive breast.

☐   Sniff the wrapping of a fresh or thawed duck for possible off odors.

☐   When cooked, a fresh duck is more tender and tasty than a frozen one.

☐   Should you have to buy a frozen duck, be sure the packaging is undamaged and the bird is firmly frozen.

☐   Because a duck is quite fatty, it has considerably less edible meat than a chicken of the same weight. A 3- to 5-pound duckling serves two diners.

☐   A duck should be thawed in the refrigerator. Allow 1 to 1½ days.

☐   Before cooking a duck, remove the excess fat near the aperture of the stomach cavity. To provide channels for the melted fat to escape as the bird roasts, pierce the skin of the duck wherever there is a thick layer of fat.

☐   To minimize the perceived fattiness of a duck, rub its skin or cavity with lemon juice before you pop it in the oven. Serve the roast duck with a sauce enriched with an acidy ingredient, such as wine or vinegar.

☐   When you stuff a duck, your goal is to flavor the duck, not to create an edible stuffing. The mixture absorbs too much fat from the duck.

☐   If cleaning a grease-splattered oven is not your idea of pleasure, cook the duck in a preheated 325-degree oven for 20 minutes plus 20 minutes per pound. Roasting the bird at a higher temperature for a shorter period, though, will produce a crisper skin.

☐   Whether you are roasting with low or high heat, basting is unnecessary. The duck has sufficient built-in fat.

☐   Before carving the duck, place it on a warm platter, cover it loosely with aluminum foil, and let it rest for about 20 minutes. The flesh will better retain its flavorful juices.

EGGPLANT

☐ The larger the eggplant is for its variety, the more bitter it will taste and the tougher its peel will be. Its ratio of seeds to edible flesh will be correspondingly high, too. Message: Buy the smallest eggplants in the bin.

☐ Eggplants should be firm, unshriveled, and heavy for their size. The skin should be free of abrasions and soft spots.

☐ Mature eggplants should be peeled. For most preparations, baby ones are best left unpeeled unless they have been waxed.

☐ The exposed flesh discolors rapidly due to oxidation. To prevent this from occurring, start cooking the eggplant as soon as it is cut. If a delay is necessary, promptly coat the surfaces with lemon juice or submerge the pieces in acidulated water.

☐ Eggplants need not be soaked in salted water to rid them of their bitterness if they are small for their variety. If the eggplants are mature, soaking helps but why buy such an eggplant in the first place?

☐ Calorie watchers should shun eggplant cooked in oil or butter because the vegetable thirstily absorbs those fats.

☐ Don't overcook eggplant in a stew lest it lose its texture by becoming waterlogged.

EGGS

Marketplace Pointers

☐ Inspect each eggshell for cracks (they could indicate bacterial contamination) and shininess (a sign that the eggs are not fresh).

HOWARD HILLMAN

☐ Contrary to popular belief, it's impossible to tell how tasty or nutritious an egg is by the color of its shell, be it brown or white.

☐ Buy large-sized eggs because virtually all recipe writers use that size as the standard of measurement.

Kitchen Hints

☐ Eggs will stay fresh longer if you store them large end up, tapered end down.

☐ The egg compartment on the refrigerator door is not an ideal storage area because the repeated temperature fluctuation and slamming of the door deteriorates the eggs. You would be better off keeping the eggs in their carton on one of the refrigerator shelves.

☐ If you forget whether a stored egg is hard cooked, spin it on the counter. Cooked eggs spin smoothly; uncooked ones wobble.

☐ Don't throw away an egg with a blood spot. Simply remove the aberration and proceed with the recipe.

☐ You can test the freshness of an egg without breaking it. Place it in a pan or bowl of cool water. If the egg floats, throw it away. If it sinks and rests on its side, it's very fresh.

☐ Cooking with a recipe that calls for only the yolk or white of the egg? Use surplus egg yolks for sauces, custards, mayonnaise, and enriched omelets. Use surplus egg whites for meringues, soufflés, frostings, and angel food cake.

☐ Soak egg-coated dirty dishes in warm, not hot or cold, water. The ideal soaking temperature is just below 156 degrees, because it's warm enough to help loosen the clinging food but not so hot that the heat sets the protein in the yolk, bonding it to the dish.

☐ Hard-cooked eggs are easier to slice if they are chilled first.

☐ *See also* Beaten Egg Whites, Fried Eggs, Hard-Cooked

(Hard-Boiled) eggs, Poached Eggs, and Scrambled Eggs and Omelets.

EMERGENCIES

☐ Should you accidentally burn yourself while cooking, immediately place the burned skin area in cold water—or under cold running water—for several minutes. This remedy reduces the pain as well as the chances of your skin blistering. Modern medicine recognizes this cold-water method as superior to the old-fashioned "rub with butter" method.

☐ Fires caused by hot oil should never be doused with water. This countermeasure would dangerously splatter and spread the flaming oil liquid. Instead, smother the fire with baking soda. (Keep a box handy for such an emergency.)

ENDIVES

☐ Buy small (young) endives because the large ones tend to be excessively bitter.

☐ The leaves should be crisp, tightly packed, and bright white, with a minimum of green surface area. You should see no yellow except at the tips. Brown spots indicate a lack of freshness.

☐ If possible, buy endives that are wrapped in tissue rather than displayed nakedly. Exposure to light increases their bitterness.

☐ For the same reason, store your endives in a closed opaque bag or container in the vegetable crisper.

☐ Quickly wash the endive with lukewarm or cold tap water as prolonged soaking produces bitterness. Pat them dry with paper towels unless you will be cooking them with moist heat promptly.

☐ Endives are usually eaten raw in salads or steamed or

braised. A not so common but gratifying alternative is stir-frying. Cut the leaves across the grain, as you would celery stalks, into ⅓-inch-wide pieces.

ENRICHED FLOUR

☐   The term "enriched" on a loaf of bread or sack of flour usually means that the miller added eight nutrients to the flour. But since the miller originally took out about 22 nutrients, he is like a thief robbing you of $22 and then "enriching" you by returning $8.

ESCAROLE

☐   This green is not a good buy if its leaves are brown-tinged or its stalks are flaccid.

☐   Escarole's curly leaves are a natural home for dirt. Wash the greens well before using them.

☐   The bitter note of escarole enlivens mixed green salads.

☐   This versatile vegetable can also be braised in butter or used as an ingredient in soup.

F

FATBACK

☐ The fatback sold in supermarkets is often extremely salty. If you think the saltiness would throw your recipe out of kilter, blanch the fatback before cooking with it.

FENNEL

☐ Buy fennel bulbs that are small, firm, and free of blemishes.
☐ Fennel's refreshing licorice flavor is best enjoyed eaten raw in salads or as a crudité. Alternatively, you can braise it or add it to stews.

Fennel Seeds. *See* Anise Seeds.

FISH

Marketplace Pointers

☐ The eyes should be as clear and bright as those of a live fish. The longer the fish is stored, the more opaque its eyes become.
☐ Sniff the fish. If it and its gills, in particular, smell fishy, decomposition is well under way.
☐ The gills reveal another clue. If the fish is fresh, the gills are bright red.
☐ Grasp the fish's head and tail and hold the body level. The fresher the fish, the less its body will sag for its size and species.
☐ Press the flesh with your fingers. If the fish is fresh, the flesh should spring back when you remove your finger.

HOWARD HILLMAN

☐ Examine the scales, if any, They should gleam, adhere tightly to the body, and be free of slime.

☐ When purchasing fish pieces, sniff the fillets and steaks for possible off odors.

☐ The longer a fillet or steak is stored, the more brown tinged and the drier the flesh becomes.

☐ If the store smells fishy, buy elsewhere. These odors indicate that the fishmonger has a slow turnover or is neglecting to keep his shop spick-and-span.

☐ If possible, don't purchase frozen fish. The difference in flavor and texture between a fresh and frozen fish is significant. The flesh of the latter becomes mushy and loses much of its flavor and nutrients when cooked.

☐ Beware of the fishmonger who sells thawed fish as fresh fish. One way to spot the ploy is to examine the cut flesh. If it is opaque rather than translucent, you are probably looking at a piece that was once frozen.

☐ If the fish is sitting in a pool of liquid, chances are it was thawed. Reason: A thawing fish loses some of its internal juices.

☐ Fat-fleshed fish should be your first choice when broiling or baking. Lean-fleshed fish is the most ideal for simmering and steaming. Should you broil or bake a lean-fleshed fish, be sure you baste it frequently.

☐ Weight watchers should note that fat-fleshed fishes are more flavorful and nutritious, but contain roughly twice the calories as lean-fleshed ones.

☐ If you don't like a lot of small bones in your whole fish, opt for ocean as opposed to freshwater fish. Ocean fish can have fewer and thicker bones, because of the buoyancy effects of salt water.

☐ Fish steaks will broil to their optimal succulence if they are approximately 1¼ inches thick.

☐ The center-cut steak is more tender and delicious than a tail cut. You can identify the center cut of a round (but not a flat) fish by its horseshoe shape.

Kitchen Hints

☐ Fish odor can be easily removed from your hands or cooking utensils by rubbing them with lemon juice. If a pot has a very pronounced fish odor, boil ½ cup of vinegar in it for a minute or two.

☐ If a medium- or large-sized fish is ungutted, gut it immediately before storing it, because pathogenic microorganisms can spread quickly through the gastronomic tract to the flesh.

☐ Fish deteriorates rapidly, even if it is frozen. Don't store the fish for more than a few days in the frozen food compartment or a month or two in the freezer.

☐ If you must use frozen fish fillets or steaks, thaw them overnight in the refrigerator, not at room temperature.

☐ The typical frozen fish sticks are not for the genuine fish lover. Not only are they made with reconstituted fish, they are bland and generously stretched with inexpensive fillers or breading.

☐ Scales are more easily removed if the fish is wet. Run cold water over the fish just before you begin the chore.

☐ A whole fish will taste better if the gills are removed before cooking it.

☐ Ditto, if you leave the head, tail, and skin on the fish. If you were to remove them, a fair share of the internal juices of the fish would drain off during the cooking process, resulting in a less flavorful and less tender flesh. (Also serve a fish intact. Its flesh will stay warm longer.)

☐ One reason why cooked fish breaks apart in the pan is that it was overhandled beforehand.

☐ The broiler must be thoroughly preheated before inserting the fish.

☐ Fish fillets need not be turned if they are broiled.

☐ Sautéed fish tends to become tough if cooked over too high or too low a heat. A moderately high setting produces the best results.

HOWARD HILLMAN

☐ Poached fish must be simmered, never boiled. Otherwise, it may fall apart.

☐ Poached fish will be whiter if you add a little vinegar, lemon juice, or white wine to the cooking liquid.

☐ If you don't have a fish poacher, wrap the fish in cheese-cloth. Use the rolled ends of the cheesecloth as handles for transferring the fish into and out of the pan.

☐ Here's a simple but accurate formula for estimating cooking time. Fish cooks in 9 minutes for each inch of maximum thickness. When poaching, start the timing as soon as the water returns to a boil. When broiling or sautéing, use moderately high heat. When baking, preheat the oven to 450 degrees.

☐ To test for doneness, use the fork test. If the flesh flakes when you probe the flesh at its thickest point, the fish is properly cooked. Further cooking will produce an undesirable mushy texture.

☐ A collaborating test is to examine the flesh as you probe it. Your fish is cooked when all of its flesh has changed from a translucent to an opaque state.

☐ Fish cooks rapidly: Be sure the serving platter and dinner plates are warmed.

☐ Turn tonight's leftover poached fish into a cold appetizer for tomorrow's dinner by marinating it overnight in the refrigerator in an oil-and-vinegar dressing.

FISH STOCK

☐ Make your fish stock from the trimmings (head, tail, and bones) of lean rather than fat-fleshed fish. The resulting stock will have a more delicate flavor, aroma, and taste.

☐ Your fish stock is less likely to become cloudy if you follow these guidelines: Use the bones and flesh of lean fish that are fresh and free of fishy odors; remove the skin and gills and wash off any blood. Gently simmer (don't boil) the stock for a maximum of 20 minutes and then promptly strain.

☐   Begin by cooking the trimmings in cold water—and simmer them for no more than 20 minutes. Further cooking develops off flavors.

☐   Your local fishmonger will usually give you trimmings free or for a nominal charge. Call the day before so that he may reserve them for you.

FLAMBÉING

☐   Kids can eat flambéed food because the heat evaporates the alcohol.

☐   Weight watchers, take note: Most of the calories in a spirit disappear as the alcohol burns off.

☐   Certain spirits and liqueurs have special affinities with certain foods. For instance, the acidity of the orange liqueurs (Grand Marnier, Cointreau, and Triple Sec) help cut the natural fattiness of duck. Apple brandy (including Calvados) pairs well with pork.

☐   The higher the proof, the more readily the spirit will burn. It should be at least 80 proof.

☐   Avoid spirits or liqueurs of mediocre quality. Your dish will taste only as good as its building blocks.

☐   Most spirits and liqueurs don't flame readily at room temperature. Warm the potent to approximately 120 degrees (slightly higher than lukewarm).

☐   Your spirit or liqueur will not flambé to its full potential if you pour it over a sauced food. A sauce dilutes the alcohol and, thereby, prematurely extinguishes the flames.

☐   Use small amounts. The spirit or liqueur should enhance, not overwhelm, your creation.

☐   Don't blow out the flames. If you don't give the alcohol a chance to burn off fully, the raw taste of alcohol can mar a dish. Moreover, blowing out the flames is unhygienic.

HOWARD HILLMAN

FLOUR

Marketplace Pointers

☐ The best wheat flour is stone ground. The product that is ground with steel rollers is less nutritious and has less flavor.

☐ Self-rising flour is little more than flour that has been given a touch of baking powder and a steep rise in price. Not only will you save money if you blend your own, your flour can be adapted for any recipe.

☐ With few exceptions, baker's flour is the best for making bread, and cake flour is preferable for making cakes. All-purpose flour is usually a poor compromise for these preparations.

☐ Your breads and other baked items will have better texture and flavor if you buy flour that hasn't been bleached. (Read the label.)

Kitchen Hints

☐ Baked items made with whole wheat flour are more nutritious, have more fiber, and have a more interesting texture. On the other hand, white flour has its assets. The resulting baked items rise to greater heights and have a more delicate flavor, which is preferable in some instances, such as when making cakes.

☐ Modern dry flour should not be sifted by the cook unless the recipe specifies sifting.

☐ The more gluten in a flour, the higher the dough will rise.

☐ White flour is best stored in a tightly sealed glass jar to keep out its three biggest enemies: moisture, air, and pests.

☐ Whole wheat flour (and other whole grain flours, such as rye) become rancid quickly. Slow down the developing rancidity by storing the flour in an airtight container in the refrigerator.

☐ However, when using refined whole grain flour for a yeast-leavened recipe, bring it to room temperature. Otherwise, the chilled flour will inhibit the yeast's growth.

□ If your flour has been stored for a long period, you may have to reduce the amount of flour and/or increase the quantity of water in a recipe. Reason: The flour may have shrunk and lost some of its moisture during storage.

FLOWERS

□ Providing that they have not been sprayed with insecticides, you can use your homegrown roses and other flowers to decorate your dishes. The petals of a flower—including those of the young carnations and dandelions—can be used as edible garnishes.

FREEZERS

□ Should a power blackout occur, don't open the freezer door, not even for one quick peek. If the freezer is reasonably filled to near capacity and not exposed to a blast of room temperature, the stored food should stay frozen for at least a day in most circumstances.

FREEZING FOODS

□ The more salt you use in a dish, the shorter the time you can safely freeze the preparation. Reason: Salt lowers the freezing point of food.

□ Give hot food in a container a chance to cool before you finally put on the lid. Otherwise, the trapped hot air in the container will allow certain spoilage-causing bacteria to proliferate and, thereby, shorten the effective storage period.

□ Don't attempt to store food in a frozen food compartment for as long as you would in a freezer. The average temperature

HOWARD HILLMAN

is 0 degrees for the latter, compared to 20 degrees for the former. A steak that would keep for several months in a freezer should not be stored more than a couple of weeks in a frozen food compartment.

☐ Air inside a package causes oxidation, damaging flavor. Wrap the food tightly, leaving a minimum of air space.

☐ One of the most common errors made when freezing foods is not labeling the package with a brief description of its contents and the date. Though it seems impossible that you'll forget that memorable dish you cooked today, time plays havoc on memory.

☐ Placing too great a volume of unfrozen food into a freezer at one time will shorten the storage life of the foods already in the unit. Before adding a new batch of food, be sure that all the previously stored food is frozen solid.

☐ If you must add a large amount of food at one time, lower the temperature of your freezer the day before. Reset it to normal the day after you've added the new food.

☐ To hasten the freezing process, leave an inch or two of space between the containers holding the unfrozen food for at least a full day.

☐ Cooked meat pieces will be juicier and more tender when thawed and reheated if they are frozen in their sauce. This partially explains why stews fare better in the freezer than, say, a broiled steak.

☐ If a food has been partially thawed, it can be safely refrozen if ice crystals are still visible.

FRENCH FRIES

☐ Use fresh vegetable oil that has a relatively high smoking point (at least 400 degrees). Safflower oil and most peanut oils fill the bill.

☐ Preheat the oil to 365 degrees, because too low a temperature produces greasy fries and too high a temperature will overcook the spud exteriors by the time the interiors are properly cooked.

☐   Use Idaho or other russet potatoes to make french fries. New potatoes are too moist and waxy.

☐   Soak the potatoes in cold water for about 15 minutes to help rid them of their starchy surface layer. Then, to prevent splatter, thoroughly pat them dry before deep-frying them.

☐   Don't crowd the pan or add too many potatoes at the same time lest you lower the cooking temperature.

☐   As soon as you remove the potatoes, pat them dry with paper towels to rid them of surface oil.

☐   French fries are best if they are eaten promptly. If a delay is necessary, you can keep them in a preheated 250-degree oven, but their quality will start depreciating markedly after about 10 minutes.

☐   An alternative to french fried potatoes are french fried potato balls. Scoop out potato spheres with a standard melon baller and deep-fry them as you would normal fries. Serve, speared with toothpicks.

FRIED EGGS

☐   The whites of fried eggs will become rubbery if you cook the eggs over high heat.

☐   Your egg whites will be rubbery if you attempt to fry the eggs "sunny side up" until the yolk firms. If you don't like runny yolks, either cook the eggs "over easy" or cover the skillet to let the trapped steam cook the top of the yolks.

FROGS' LEGS

☐   If the frogs' legs have an off odor or a noticeably moist surface, they are not fresh.

☐   Another test for freshness is to press the flesh with your fingertip. The flesh of the frog should spring back when you release the pressure.

☐   If you suspect that the frogs' legs may be on the tough side, soak them in milk for a couple of hours.

☐   If you buy frozen frogs' legs, make certain that the container is frozen completely and is not sticky. Thaw the package overnight in the refrigerator.

☐   Most people overcook frogs' legs and, consequently, end up with an unnecessarily tough entrée. Sautéing them for several minutes is usually adequate.

FRUIT

☐   Chances are that the fruit you buy in today's marketplace won't be ready to eat immediately. By letting the fruit ripen further, it becomes sweeter, because more of its starch content will have been converted into sugar. In addition, the fruit will seem sweeter, because it loses some of its acidity during the ripening process.

☐   To ripen apples, peaches, pears, and most other common fruits, store them in a pierced brown bag at room temperature until ripe, allowing one to several days.

☐   Once ripened, the fruit should be eaten promptly or stored in the refrigerator crisper or in a cool, dark place.

☐   When refrigerating fruits and vegetables for up to a few days, keep them sealed in a plastic bag. This retards moisture loss. It also inhibits the transfer of odors between foods. (If a longer refrigeration period is necessary, the bag should be pierced.)

☐   Do not wash fruits and vegetables until just before you start preparing them. Otherwise, the added moisture will hasten bacterial spoilage.

☐   Convert your very ripe but still fresh fruits, such as peaches and strawberries, into a thick sauce for topping ice cream and other desserts.

☐   Give your fresh fruit salad a little extra spirit with a sprinkling of orange liqueur.

☐   *See also* other fruit entries, such as Apple, Mango, and Kiwis.

FUNNEL

☐   Every kitchen should have a wide-mouthed funnel for transferring foods, such as nuts and dried beans, from a package into a jar.

G

Game. *See* Guinea Fowl and Squab.

GARLIC

Marketplace Pointers

☐ Avoid garlic powder and garlic salt. Their taste is abominable. Also, forget about the minced garlic-in-oil products because they have (or soon develop) a bitter flavor.

☐ The whole garlic that is sold loose in a bin is usually much fresher than those merchandised in small paper boxes. Under no circumstances should you consider buying packaged garlic that contains the cloves already separated; they probably will be over the hill by the time you take them home.

☐ If you want to buy the strongest flavored of the widely sold types of garlic, buy the small, rose-skinned variety. Next in strength comes the violet-skinned strains. The oversized elephant strain is the mildest.

☐ One advantage of the over-sized garlic cloves is that they require less peeling time than the smaller ones on an ounce-per-ounce basis.

☐ Squeeze the garlic. It should feel firm and not be shriveled. Soft spots indicate internal decay.

☐ Lift the garlic. The bulb should be heavy for its size. Lightness suggests partial dehydration and internal decay.

☐ Rub the garlic. It's probably past its prime if the papery outer layers crinkle and fall off readily.

Kitchen Hints

☐ Garlic is best stored in a cool, dark, well-ventilated spot. Should you refrigerate it, at least be sure to seal it tightly in a plastic bag to prevent it from decaying prematurely and giving off and absorbing odors.

☐ One way to save preparation time is to peel the garlic as soon as you bring it home. Place the whole peeled cloves in a jar, cover them with olive or other cooking oil, and refrigerate. Use as needed. The garlic should keep fresh for at least a couple of weeks, as long as it has not been sliced, chopped, or minced.

☐ Cloves are easier to peel if you first blanch them in boiling water for about 10 seconds. Keep that in mind the next time you have to prepare a large batch of garlic.

☐ Think twice about cooking with whole garlic cloves if you purchased them in a store; many such specimens have rotten cores or have a developing sprout (which can turn bitter when sautéed). It's generally wise to at least cut each clove in half so that you can spot those shortcomings and, if necessary, remove them.

☐ The garlic will stick less to the blade of your chopping knife if you sprinkle salt on the garlic. Just be sure to reduce the quantity of salt called for in the recipe. (A side benefit is that the salt absorbs the garlic flavor that would normally be lost to the board.)

☐ If you are concerned about the garlic leaving an odor on your cutting board and your recipe calls for both garlic and parsley, chop the garlic first. Then, on the same spot, chop the parsley. The chlorophyll in the parsley will neutralize the garlic scent.

☐ A lightly crushed garlic clove adds an interesting background note to marinades. It's easily discarded when the marinating has been completed.

☐ For a hint of garlic in your salad, rub the salad bowl with a crushed garlic clove and then discard it.

☐ Garlic will scorch and, therefore, become bitter if you add it to the sauté pan at the same time you add the onion. Unlike onions, garlic cannot successfully be sautéed for more than a minute. If the oil is very hot, 30 seconds is the limit.

HOWARD HILLMAN

GARLIC PRESS

☐ The garlic press is one of the worst culinary gadgets. The extracted juices can quickly turn bitter in hot oil or butter. It's also a time-consuming nuisance to clean the tool, and if you don't wash it thoroughly, the lingering garlic oil will turn rancid and develop an off odor that can be transferred to future preparations.

GARNISHES

☐ The right garnish in discreet quantities can transform an ordinary looking dish into an eye-catching presentation. One key to success is contrast, be it color, shape, or texture.
☐ Keep this list of easy to obtain garnishes handy as a quick reminder: strips of cheese, ham, fresh ginger, pimiento, sweet peppers or scallions; whole cherries, tomatoes, mushroom caps, anchovies, smoked oysters, arctic shrimp, olives, capers, or gherkins; sprigs of dill, watercress, basil, or coriander leaves; slices of tomato, mushroom, hard-cooked eggs, orange, grapefruit, kiwi, or olives; crumbled egg yolks; or chopped egg whites.

GAS BURNER

☐ If the flame of your gas burner displays too much yellow, you are wasting fuel energy. Adjust the burner's air vent until the flame is virtually all blue.

GELATIN

☐ You need not restrict yourself to the standard gelatin flavors sold in supermarkets. Create your own special gelatins by using an unflavored gelatin mixture made with the fresh fruit of your choice. Have you tried mango gelatin?

☐   You know that you are using too high a proportion of gelatin to liquid, if your finished preparation has a rubbery texture or surface. Measure accurately.

☐   If you increase the quantity of acid or sugar called for in a gelatin mixture recipe, you will also have to add more gelatin or less water to the mixture. Acid and sugar hinder the thickening process.

☐   Your gelatin preparation may end up lumpy unless you stir the mixture an hour or so before it fully sets. The gelatin mixture near the bottom and the side of the dish has a tendency to become lumpy because it solidifies long before the liquid in the center. By stirring, you minimize this problem.

☐   If the prepared gelatin is stuck in its mold, turn the mold over in the serving dish. Drape a warm towel over the mold for several seconds or until the gelatin loosens.

☐   If you have trouble positioning an unmolded gelatin preparation in the center of a serving dish, your task will be easier if you lightly moisten the platter with cold tap water beforehand.

☐   Give your leftover gelatin a new personality by incorporating other non-liquid ingredients into it. Simply reheat the gelatin; add the new ingredients and refrigerate for at least several hours.

GIBLETS

☐   Remove the giblets from the cavity of an unfrozen bird as soon as you bring them home from the store. These parts spoil rapidly and can contaminate the rest of the chicken.

☐   The quick way to assess freshness is to sniff the giblets. If they have the slightest off odor or if they are off colored, discard them.

☐   The younger the bird, the more tender and delectable the liver and gizzard are. However, even the giblets of a young bird will become tough if overcooked.

☐   If you've cooked the liver to the point where all traces of its internal pinkness have disappeared, it is overdone.

GIFTS

☐ Save those foreign beer bottles that come with attached porcelain caps. When you have saved enough of them, buy a gallon of a virgin Italian olive oil. Divide it into the various bottles and give them as gifts.

GINGER

☐ Fresh ginger will only be as good as it smells. Give it the sniff test.
☐ Leave fresh ginger in the greengrocer's bin if it is bruised, cracked, moldy, or shriveled.
☐ Powdered ginger is a horrendous substitute for the fresh product. Don't ruin a dish by using it.
☐ Fresh peeled ginger can be stored for several weeks if submerged in dry sherry in a covered glass jar in the refrigerator.
☐ Fish is often cooked with ginger because that flavoring agent helps counteract fishy odors.

GOOSE

☐ Examine the shape of the breast; it should be plump and meaty and bisymmetrical.
☐ The younger the goose, the more tender the meat. Look for a specimen that is small for its variety.
☐ Geese have a lot of fat, so figure on at least 1 pound of dressed goose per diner. On holiday occasions, use the 1½ to 2 pounds per guest formula.
☐ There's no need to baste a roasting goose with oil or butter—it has enough natural fat to do the job automatically.
☐ Roast an unstuffed goose in a preheated 375-degree oven for 20 minutes plus 20 minutes per pound. (Add 4 minutes per

pound if the goose is stuffed.) For a crisp skin, raise the oven temperature to 400 degrees ½ hour before completion. Curtail the overall cooking period by 5 minutes—but be forewarned that this technique increases grease splatter in your oven.

☐ Stuffing a goose with ingredients, such as lemon wedges, prunes, apples, and parsley will heighten the flavor of the meat. Any stuffing, however, will absorb a lot of fat from the bird during the cooking process and, therefore, is best discarded.

GRAHAM CRACKERS

☐ Graham crackers can lose their firm texture if you don't store them in an airtight container once you open the package.

GRAPEFRUITS

☐ When confronted with a bin of grapefruits, search for a well-proportioned fruit. Its skin should be free of bruises and blemishes, and be thin and smooth rather than thick and spongy. When squeezed, it should feel firm yet resilient.

☐ Store grapefruits in a cool, dark, well-ventilated spot for several days. For longer periods, keep them in a sealed plastic bag in your vegetable crisper.

☐ A grapefruit half will sit more steadily on a plate if you slice off ¼ inch of its round bottom.

☐ The custom of sprinkling sugar on grapefruit should be shelved nowadays because grapefruits (at least the good ones) are sweeter than they used to be.

☐ The next time you poach a white-fleshed fish, add a touch of freshly squeezed grapefruit juice to the simmering water. The grapefruit adds flavor and helps keep the flesh white. (Reserve a few segments of the grapefruit to use as a garnish.)

GRAPEFRUIT SPOON

☐ Most of the culinary gadgets sold in today's gourmet marketplace are silly tools. One of the exceptions is the grapefruit spoon. (The tip is pointed and one or both edges are serrated.) Buy a set for your family.

GRAPE LEAVES

☐ Fresh grape leaves are immeasurably superior to the bottled or canned products, which are quite salty.

☐ When buying fresh grape leaves, look for those that are untorn and relatively small.

☐ If you must use canned or bottled grape leaves, be sure to rinse and soak them thoroughly in lukewarm water to rid them of their excess salinity.

☐ Most cooks use grape leaves only for making dolmas (rice or rice-and-lamb-stuffed grape leaves). Experiment, for instance, by stuffing the leaves with feta cheese cubes and chopped prosciutto.

GRAPES

☐ The first grapes of the season for any specific variety are usually too tart for pleasant eating. Wait a few weeks.

☐ If you do sample a grape in the store, wipe it off thoroughly with a moistened tissue. Most grape vines are well sprayed with insecticides and fungicides.

☐ Pick up a bunch of grapes. The individual fruits should be plump to the point where they seem to be bursting out of their skins. There should be no cracks, soft spots, or discoloration.

☐ If the grapes can be pulled off easily (or if there are loose grapes in the box), the grapes have been stored too long.

☐ The stems should be pliable and green rather than stiff and brown.

☐ Grapes sold in bunches out of a box are usually in better condition than the prepackaged variety. And—as a bonus— you get to pick and choose.

☐ Because surface moisture hastens bacterial attack, don't wash the grapes before you are ready to eat them.

☐ Store the grapes along with a dry sheet of paper towel (to absorb moisture) in a plastic bag in the vegetable crisper.

☐ Cold grapes can be refreshing on a scorching day, but to be able to enjoy their full flavor, serve them at approximately 60 degrees, just below room temperature.

GREEN BEANS

☐ A green or waxed bean is not fresh unless it snaps when you break it in half.

☐ The skin should be unblemished and a vivid green.

☐ The younger the green bean, the more tender it is.

☐ Store green beans, unwashed, sealed in a plastic bag in the vegetable crisper for a maximum of several days.

☐ Raw, young, prime-condition green beans make a nutritious crudité or salad ingredient. To heighten their color, you may want to blanch them for roughly 10 seconds.

☐ Cook twice as many green beans as you intend to serve at a meal. While the green beans are still hot, toss half of them in a seasoned vinegar and oil dressing. Refrigerate and serve the marinated green beans as a cold vegetable side dish within the next few days.

Green Onions. *See* Scallions.

HOWARD HILLMAN

GROUND BEEF

Marketplace Pointers

☐   For hamburgers, buy ground chuck, not ground round or sirloin. Your burgers will be more tasty because the meat is more flavorful to begin with. They will also be juicier because the extra fat in ground chuck keeps the meat moist as it cooks. You needn't be overly concerned about the extra fat should you be watching your weight, because most of that substance drains out of the meat by the time the burger is cooked.

☐   Ground round is a better choice than ground chuck for meatloaf, because it has less fat. Unlike in the case for burgers, the fat does not drain out of the preparation during cooking. It is absorbed by the breadcrumbs and other meatloaf ingredients.

☐   Ground round is a better choice than ground sirloin for meatloaf because this preparation needs more fat than ground sirloin normally has. Ground round also provides more flavor than ground sirloin.

☐   The hue of the meat is a reliable indicator of freshness. Freshly ground beef is bright, rosy red. As it sits in the meat case, the meat gradually turns brown.

☐   Buy ground beef only for short-term consumption. It is quite perishable because most of its mass is exposed to the air during the grinding process.

Kitchen Hints

☐   Your ground beef will be juicier and more tender when cooked if you chop the meat in your food processor rather than buying it preground at the store. The latter meat is somewhat pasty, because it has been pressed through the small holes in the grinding machine.

☐   When using a food processor, don't overchop the meat or

you will be doing as much damage as the butcher does with a supermarket grinder.

☐ Leaden hamburgers are partially the result of over-handling the meat before it is cooked. Don't start mixing until you assemble all the herbs, spices, salt, pepper, and other seasonings on top of the meat in the bowl. Then blend lightly. Further mixing will make the meat pasty.

☐ If your hamburger is to be succulent, it should be shaped reasonably thick. Try to tell this to the large national hamburger fast-food outlets.

☐ The cooking pan and, if broiling, the broiler, must be preheated if the meat is to sear properly. A preheated cooking pan also minimizes sticking.

☐ Substitute crusty french bread or hard rolls for storebought hamburger buns, which tend to be bland and cottony.

Ground Pepper. *See* Peppercorns.

GUINEA FOWL

☐ Guinea fowl is a much more difficult bird to cook than chicken. The slightest overcooking dries its flesh, making it stringy. Baste the bird often and, as an added precaution, bard it.

☐ Choose a hen rather than a male. Its extra fat helps keep the flesh moist as the meat cooks.

H

HAM

Marketplace Pointers

☐ Food processors put their best ham in their larger cans. The contents of their smaller cans usually comprise bits, pieces, or small chunks of meat that have been pressed together.

☐ You may be paying more money per pound of ham than you think if you buy a ham with the words "added water" and "natural juices" printed on the label. These terms mean that the ham weighs up to 10 percent more than its original weight because of the addition of liquid.

☐ The canned hams that say "need no refrigeration" can be stored on unrefrigerated shelves because the processor cooked the meat excessively. As a result, the products will never taste as good as the canned ham requiring refrigeration.

☐ When buying a whole ham that is not in a can, choose a small specimen. The smaller the leg, the younger the animal, and, therefore, the more tender and delectable the flesh will be.

☐ The shorter the shank end is, relative to the whole ham, the more meat and less bone waste you'll get.

Kitchen Hints

☐ Keep on hand, a small hunk of boned cooked ham in your freezer. When you need a small quantity of diced ham to flavor a preparation, such as an omelet or a stew, cut off a ¼-inch-thick slice and dice it. Rewrap and return the unused ham to the freezer for future use.

☐   Though a canned ham labeled "ready-to-eat" is indeed safe to eat, the meat should be heated thoroughly even if you plan to eat it cold. This radically improves the flavor.

☐   Ham slices that are between ¾ and 1½ inches thick are best broiled. Pan-broil thinner and oven-bake thicker ones.

☐   Should you wish to stud your ham with cloves, insert them at or near the end of the cooking process. Otherwise, the cloves' flavor will be overwhelming. Don't forget to remove them before slicing, as biting into them can break a tooth.

☐   Glaze the ham fat side up. The luster of the caramelized coating appears more striking on fat than on flesh.

☐   Remove the skin from a ham soon after it is cooked. The task becomes increasingly difficult as the meat cools.

☐   Your ham slices will be more tender if you slice them as thinly as your knife will allow. Slice across the grain (perpendicular to the bone).

Hamburgers. *See* Ground Beef.

HARD-COOKED (HARD-BOILED) EGGS

☐   The best way to hard-cook an egg is to remove it from the refrigerator and pierce the center of its larger end with a push pin or other sharp point in order to keep the egg from cracking when it cooks. Then, submerge the egg in rapidly boiling water. Lower the heat to a simmer and cook for 12 to 15 minutes, depending on your preference. Promptly submerge the egg in cold water to stop the cooking process, because further cooking could produce a sulfurous odor and a green-tinged yolk.

☐   For soft-boiled eggs, use the above recipe, but cook for only 5 to 7 minutes and skip the cooling step.

☐   A fresh from-the-coop egg is harder to peel than one seven days old. Your peeling job will be easier if you begin the task before the egg has completely cooled. Doing it under cold running water helps, as does starting at the large end of the egg.

HASHBROWNS

☐   Gently turn hashbrowns. If you compress them with a spatula, you'll semi-mash the flesh, ruining the texture and smoothing the sharp edges, which help give the preparation its visual appeal.

HEALTH AND NUTRITION

☐   Don't cut or peel fruits and vegetables too far ahead of time. Once their flesh is exposed to the air, they lose nutrients (and flavor) quickly.

☐   The cardinal rule for cooking vegetables is to use as little water and as short a cooking time as possible.

☐   Use the leftover cooking water as a base for soups.

☐   Vegetarians should make it a point to serve legumes (beans, peas, peanuts, etc.) with cereal grains (such as wheat, rice or corn) at the same meal. The combination provides your body with all of the eight essential amino acids found in meat.

☐   Don't taste-test a suspect food until you have given it the eye and nose tests. In more than 95 percent of the cases, the combination of those two senses will detect unwholesomeness and, thereby, will spare you having to sample the food.

☐   "When in doubt, throw it out" is one of the soundest of culinary maxims.

HEART

☐   Figuratively and physically, hearts toughen as a mammal ages. Buy young specimens.

☐   Don't buy the heart if its red flesh is beginning to turn brown or if it has developed an off odor.

□   A heart is especially prone to toughening if it is over-cooked. Because it is a well-used muscle, it is best when braised slowly.

HERB BREAD

□   Like garlic bread? Then, you'll enjoy herb bread, too. Cut a loaf of french bread crosswise into 1-inch-thick slices. Brush the cut surfaces with a mixture of olive oil, thyme, and minced scallions. Reassemble and wrap the loaf in aluminum foil and warm it in a preheated 375-degree oven for 12 to 15 minutes.

HERBS AND SPICES

Marketplace Pointers

□   Fresh herbs should be bright green and aromatic. Reject them if you see browning or wilting, or smell even the slightest sourness.

□   Dried herbs will never be as vividly hued as fresh herbs, but they still should be reasonably verdant. They should also have a pronounced refreshing aroma.

□   Whole spices are more aromatic than preground ones; they also have appreciably longer storage lives.

□   If you do buy preground spices for the sake of convenience, buy very small amounts.

□   The dried herbs and spices sold in cellophane packages may not be as fresh as they should be because cellophane lets in the air. Better containers are tins and glass jars.

□   Some specialty stores sell dried herbs and spices by the ounce out of oversized jars. Be sure that the store has a rapid turnover, because the frequent opening and closing of the jars exposes the supply to repeated doses of air and moisture. Light also can do damage to herbs and spices stored on shelves in glass containers.

HOWARD HILLMAN

☐ Don't buy those herb and spice containers that have cork stoppers. Air can easily seep through cork.

Kitchen Hints

☐ Fresh herbs, such as parsley, mint, dill, and coriander leaves, will stay fresh longer if you refrigerate them in a covered jar with their stem ends sitting in a 1-inch layer of water. Alternatively, wrap the stem ends with a moist paper towel and seal them in a plastic bag in the refrigerator.

☐ Sometimes we purchase more fresh herbs than we can use. One method of putting them to good use is to make herb vinegar. Submerge the washed and dried herbs in a plain quality vinegar in a glass jar and refrigerate. When the herbs begin to discolor, strain the vinegar back into its original bottle and store it in a cool, dark place. Discard the herbs.

☐ Another way to preserve surplus fresh herbs is to make herb butter. Cream the butter and herbs on a 10 to 1 basis. Form the mixture into a 1-inch-thick log and freeze it. When ready to use, slice ⅛-inch-thick rounds off the log and place them on top of preparations such as grilled steaks and vegetable dishes. As the herb butter melts, it flavors the food.

☐ Yet another way to preserve fresh herbs is to heat them in a single layer on a baking sheet in a preheated 200-degree oven until they are thoroughly dry. Store the herbs whole or crushed in sealed containers in a cool, dark place.

☐ If you frequently use minced fresh herbs, save time by investing in a quality pair of scissors for snipping the herb sprigs.

☐ One of the most popular and worst places to store herbs is near the oven. What you gain in convenience, you lose in diminished aromatics. Ideally, the temperature of the storage spot should be less than 60 degrees.

☐ Storing dried herbs and spices in glass containers is acceptable as long as you keep them in a dark place.

☐   Save steps by hanging a set of measuring spoons on the side of your herb and spice rack.

☐   As a rule of thumb, dried herbs should be replaced at least every 6 months, preferably every 3 months. Consequently, the economy sized containers of dried herbs are seldom a value.

☐   Sometimes it's hard to remember how long ago you bought a certain herb or spice. As soon as you bring home the jar or cannister, write the date on a small piece of masking tape and stick it to the bottom of the container.

☐   To heighten the flavor of a spice, roast it in a single layer in a preheated 250-degree oven for 10 to 15 minutes, just before you plan to use it in a dish.

☐   Before adding dried herbs to soups, stews, and sauces, place them in the palm of your hand and crush them with the thumb of your other hand. This helps to release their aromatic oils and makes it easier for you to spot and discard unwanted stems.

☐   When substituting dried herbs for fresh ones in a recipe, use only one-third to one-half as much. When substituting fresh for dried herbs, use two to three times as much.

☐   When experimenting with a new herb or spice, it's better to scrimp than squander. Underseasoned dishes can be rectified far easier than overseasoned ones.

☐   Spices become bitter if they are cooked over high heat for more than a short period. It's wise not to add seasoning agents, such as chili powder and black pepper, at the beginning of the sautéing process.

☐   Don't boil an herb-seasoned dish because the aromatic oils of herbs are volatile. Simmer the preparation.

☐   Your slow-cooked stews and braised dishes will be more aromatic if you don't add most of the herbs until 30 minutes before the end of the cooking period.

☐   If you are cooking a food that you plan to freeze, add all or at least most of the seasonings after you thaw the food. Seasonings permanently lose much of their aromatic and flavoring strengths when they are frozen.

HONEY

☐ Calorie- and nutrition-conscious cooks, take note: One tablespoon of honey has almost as many calories as a tablespoon of sugar. Honey also provides meager nutrients; it is mainly empty calories. It's delicious, though.

☐ Your honey will remain fluid and uncrystallized if you store it in a cool, dark place rather than in the refrigerator. Be sure the lid is tightly closed.

☐ To thin and decrystallize a refrigerated honey, either leave it out overnight or place it in a pan of hot water.

☐ You can substitute honey for sugar in most recipes, but you must take into consideration several variables. Because honey is sweeter than sugar, you must use only 90 percent as much honey as you would sugar. Since honey is a liquid, reduce the liquid called for in the recipe. Honey is somewhat acidic; therefore, replace all or part of the baking powder in the recipe with baking soda.

Honeydew Melons. *See* Melons.

HORSERADISH

☐ If you love horseradish sauce, don't buy the bottled products. Any resemblance between them and the homemade version is strictly coincidental. Once grated, horseradish quickly loses its exhilarating aromatics, which are essential for off-setting the natural harsh flavor of this root.

☐ Serve freshly grated horseradish as a condiment for preparations such as braised pork or roast beef. If you add it to the pot or smear it on a roasting meat, the cooking heat will destroy much of the enticing aromatics before the diner takes his first bite.

I

ICE CREAM

Marketplace Pointers

☐ The value of an ice cream should not be judged solely on a cost-per-volume basis. Some ice creams have more air whipped into them than others. The next time you're in a supermarket, weigh both a quality and a mediocre ice cream of identical volume. Notice that the inferior brand weighs appreciably less. In effect, you will be paying for a lot of air instead of cream if you buy it.

☐ Don't think of ice milk or sherbet as low-calorie substitutes for ice cream. Though these two desserts contain less butterfat than ice cream, they have more sugar.

☐ Examine the package. If it is sticky, it probably was partially thawed and refrozen, and, thus, may have developed a crystallized texture.

☐ Squeeze the package. It should be firm.

Kitchen Hints

☐ Unless the ice cream remains frozen solid between the time you buy and serve it, tiny ice crystals will form and ruin the texture. Be sure the ice cream is the last item you put into your shopping cart. Ask for a foil-lined insulated bag. Go directly home and promptly transfer the ice cream to your freezer.

☐ If you don't have a freezer, plan to use the ice cream in a day or two. The temperature of a frozen food compartment is not cold enough for long-term storage.

☐ Ice cream can readily absorb odors. Keep the product

HOWARD HILLMAN

sealed in the insulated bag provided by the store or use a plastic bag.

□ One way to test the quality of ice cream is to notice how quickly it melts in a spoon—the slower the rate, the better the ice cream.

□ A quality ice cream will have a creamy texture. Chalkiness indicates that the producers used non-traditional thickeners to extend shelf life.

□ Every now and then, ice cream accidentally melts. Since you can't refreeze ice cream successfully, use it as a dessert sauce—on blueberry pie or fresh fruit, for instance.

□ Virtually all commercial ice cream is flavored with vanillin, artificial vanilla. If you spot tiny black specks in the ice cream, you know the producer used genuine vanilla beans.

ICE CUBES

□ A fifty-fifty mixture of ice and water in an ice bucket will chill a bottle of wine much quicker than will the ice cubes alone.

□ When adding the ice and water to the bucket, be sure to add the water first. Otherwise, the ice cubes will stick together.

□ Ice cubes easily pick up odors from the freezer that can be transferred to your beverage. To rid a cube of this surface odor, rinse the ice quickly under cold running water just before you use it.

□ Give your fruit punches and iced teas a colorful touch by freezing a small garnish, such as a blueberry or cooked cranberry, within each ice cube.

□ Your ice cubes will be sparkling clear for your parties if you use bottled spring water to make them.

ICED TEA

☐ Iced tea tastes best if you brew it using the cold-water method. Place the tea leaves (and sugar, lemon peel, and mint, if you like) in a jar filled with cold water. Cover and refrigerate overnight without stirring the mixture. Lightly stir, strain, and serve.

☐ *See also* Tea.

Ice Milk. *See* Ice Cream.

ICING

☐ To make icing, use confectioners sugar. Because it is more finely ground, it better blends into the icing mixture.

☐ *See also* Sugar.

J

JAMS AND JELLIES

☐ The higher-priced jam or jelly may be the better bargain than an inexpensive one; because its natural fruit flavor is more intense, you won't have to use as much to appreciate its flavor.
☐ Once opened, jams and jellies will stay fresher longer in the refrigerator than at room temperature.

JARS AND BOTTLES

☐ If a jar or bottle won't open, don't pound the side of the lid. This makes matters worse. Instead, pound the top of the lid flatly on the floor or another hard surface.
☐ To prevent cracking, warm a glass storage jar or bottle with hot water before transferring hot foods or liquids into it.

JERUSALEM ARTICHOKES

☐ Buy small specimens. The skin should be unblemished and the scent fresh. Be on the alert for signs of mold.
☐ Store whole Jerusalem artichokes (sunchokes) in a sealed plastic bag in the vegetable crisper for up to a week.
☐ Scrub the skin well, to dislodge the dirt hidden in the recesses of this knobby vegetable.
☐ Though this tuber is usually peeled, its skin is nutritious.
☐ Jerusalem artichokes are at their best in terms of flavor and texture if they are eaten raw. Add bite-sized pieces to salads or serve them in chunks to be dipped in a seasoned oil and vinegar sauce.
☐ Steamed Jerusalem artichoke cubes make a perfect base for tomato sauces.

K

KALE

☐ Kale can be tender and delicate or fibrous and assertive, depending on whether the plant is, respectively, young or mature.

☐ Look for small, unwilted, vividly hued leaves with semi-firm midribs.

☐ Unless the kale is very young, the midribs should be removed before you cook the vegetable. The stalks should always be removed no matter what the plant's maturity, but in the case of young kale, they can be enjoyed if they are cooked separately or given a head start in the pan.

☐ Like spinach, young kale leaves need only brief cooking; they respond well to steaming and sautéing.

Ketchup. *See* Condiments.

KIDNEYS

☐ Kidneys from young animals taste best. They have more delectable textures and can be cooked with dry heat, such as broiling. Age can be detected by the color: The paler the kidney for its species, the younger the animal.

☐ Kidneys are quite perishable. The flesh should glisten and be firm and free of off odors.

☐ A kidney will broil crisper if you don't wash it. Reason: Kidneys absorb water readily.

HOWARD HILLMAN

KIWIS

☐ Kiwis will display a striking geometric design if you slice them crosswise rather than lengthwise.

☐ Try rubbing pork chops with a cut kiwi before you cook them. The fruit will help to tenderize the meat. (Save the reserved portion of the kiwi to garnish the finished dish.)

KNIVES

☐ Wooden handles are less likely to slip in your hand than plastic or nylon ones, especially when they are moist or greasy.

☐ Magnetic knife holders can be dangerous, especially after a year's use, when the bar begins to lose its magnetic power.

☐ Another bad place to store your kitchen knives is in a drawer. They can bang against each other, dulling their cutting edges.

☐ The best storage device is a wooden wall rack or counter stand.

☐ Make it a habit to sharpen a knife with a butcher's steel every time you remove it from the storage rack. Ten or so strokes should be adequate if you perform this task religiously.

☐ Occasionally, you may need to use a carbon or diamond stone but never use a grinding stone. The latter can wear away the blade of your knife within a few years. (A quality knife should outlive you.)

☐ If you want to transport your kitchen knives, a free and handy case can be made from the cardboard tube from a roll of aluminum foil, wax paper, plastic wrap, or paper towels. Flatten the tube, seal one end with a durable tape, insert the knife point first, and close the open end of the tube with tape.

KOHLRABI

☐ You'll be buying the best of kohlrabi if it is relatively small (young) and has vivid green leaves still attached to the stalks protruding from the bulb. The skin should be thin and free of cuts, discoloration, and soft spots.

☐   Kohlrabi can be eaten raw or cooked, but it must be peeled before eating.

☐   Typically, kohlrabi is stewed, sliced, cubed, or cut into julienne.

☐   Dill and caraway seeds partner well with kohlrabi—ask any Scandinavian.

L

LABEL REMOVAL

☐ Soak the glass jar in hot detergent water, overnight if necessary.

☐ If that fails, and it is essential to rid the jar of its label, boil the jar in detergent water.

☐ As a last resort, soak the jar overnight in alcohol or paint thinner in a safe, well-ventilated place.

LAMB

Marketplace Pointers

☐ The younger the animal, the more tender its flesh and the less muttony the flavor.

☐ Clues to age include the color of the flesh and fat. As the animal ages, its flesh loses its paleness and its white fat picks up a yellow tint. That fat gradually develops a dry, crumbly texture.

☐ Other useful age indicators are the bones (they gradually harden) and the relative size of the cut.

☐ The degree of tenderness is also determined by the cut (shoulder chops are tougher than loin chops), the grade (USDA Prime is the best), and whether the meat was frozen (the freezing process negatively affects tenderness).

☐ Look for firm, fine-grained flesh that still has a fresh glow.

☐ A whole leg of lamb should be plump. Scrawny legs have a lower meat-to-fat-and-bone ratio.

☐ When buying a half leg of lamb, you face a dilemma. The sirloin butt half is more tender but yields less meat per pound of weight and is more difficult to carve than the shank half.

☐ For optimum succulence, your lamb chops should be at least 1½ inches thick.

☐ The bones infuse flavor into the flesh as the meat cooks, so think twice about buying a boned lamb roast.

Kitchen Hints

☐ Lamb will smell and taste less "lamby" if you trim off the excess fat before broiling, sautéing, or roasting it.

☐ Lamb toughens and loses much of its subtle flavor when it is overcooked. You know the meat has reached this stage when the color of the interior of the flesh changes from pink to brown.

☐ For rare roasted lamb, remove the meat from the oven when its internal temperature registers 125 degrees. Add 10 degrees for medium-rare and another 10 degrees for medium roasted lamb.

☐ Some cooks automatically insert a congregation of garlic cloves into a lamb roast. Sadly, this technique produces monotonous fare. It also has a toughening effect on the cooking meat, as it provides channels for the internal juices to escape.

☐ Slice a leg of lamb across the grain of the meat (perpendicular to the bone). Cutting the meat with the grain (parallel to the bone) produces tougher and chewier slices.

LARD

☐ Lard is a better fat to use than butter or margarine for piecrusts, because it produces the lightest and flakiest texture.

☐ When substituting lard for butter or margarine in a recipe, decrease the measurement by one-quarter.

☐ You can accurately measure lard with the displacement method. Suppose your recipe calls for one-third cup of lard. Fill a measuring cup one-third full with water. Then, keep adding lard to it until the water reaches the two-thirds level.

LEEKS

☐ Immature leeks are the most tender and delicate tasting. Older leeks usually have fibrous textures and assertive flavors. Signs of overage include a thick stem and a relatively large protruding ring (the developing bulb) just above the rootlets.

☐ The leaves are the best indication of freshness. If they are flabby, yellow tinged, withered, or have lost their bright green hue, they have been around too long.

☐ The white stem should be long for the size of the leek. It should not be marred or discolored.

☐ For the sake of aesthetics and even cooking, buy equal-sized leeks.

☐ Store leeks in a sealed plastic bag in the vegetable crisper.

☐ Leeks have a lot of sand and grit ensconced between their tightly packed leaves. Wash the cut portions well in lukewarm water before cooking them.

☐ Don't toss the fibrous tops into the garbage. Use them to flavor soups, stocks, and stews.

LEFTOVERS

☐ If a food needs to be refrigerated, don't give bacteria a chance to proliferate by letting the leftovers sit on your dining room table longer than necessary.

☐ Whenever you have a leftover, such as cauliflower, that you can't seem to find a use for, think blender or food processor. Chances are better than fifty-fifty that you can purée it for flavoring and thickening a soup. Or you can chop or mince the food, turning it into a sauce for rice or pasta. Or you can combine the leftovers with scrambled eggs for a brunch dish.

☐ You can also use the chopped or minced leftovers for making croquettes. For each cup of solids, you need about ½ cup of prepared cream sauce. Mix the two ingredients together, form into balls, coat them with beaten eggs (optional) and bread crumbs, and let sit at room temperature for 20 to 30 minutes before deep-frying them.

☐ Leftover meats can toughen and leftover vegetables can soften when you reheat them. To minimize the loss in texture, bring a leftover dish to room temperature. Then thoroughly heat the sauce and other liquid components of the dish before you add the meat and, then, the vegetables. Serve the dish the minute it is heated through.

☐ Freezing zaps the flavor of prepared dishes, especially if they have been seasoned with herbs and spices. Once thawed, these preparations need to be reseasoned (but not resalted). Alternatively, prepare a seasoned but unsalted sauce for the food.

☐ Overcooking leftovers robs them of their flavor. If they are still wholesome, reheat them slowly just to the point where they are hot throughout.

LEMONS

☐ Spongy, thick-skinned lemons offer less juice than their firm, thin-skinned counterparts. The same is true for lemons that have pitted rather than smooth skins.

☐ Buy lemons that are full-shaped and heavy for their size.

☐ Examine the bulb on the end of the lemon. The smaller the protuberance, the less mature and, therefore, the less full-flavored the fruit is likely to be.

☐ Smell the lemon. It should have a fresh characteristic scent. A fermented smell or no smell are negative signs.

☐ Keep lemons in sealed plastic bags in the vegetable crisper. However, for short-term storage (a maximum of several days), you can store the fruit uncovered in a cool, dark, well-ventilated place.

☐ Once squeezed, use the juice promptly as it loses its desirable aromatics quickly. The same goes for grated lemon rind.

HOWARD HILLMAN

☐ Bring lemons to room temperature before you squeeze them. This increases the amount of juice you can extract.

☐ Need only a few drops from a whole lemon? Save the lemon for future use by making a deep, X-shaped incision into the fruit with the point of a paring knife. Squeeze out the juice you need and store the fruit sealed in plastic wrap in the refrigerator.

☐ Scrub lemons well before using them to garnish foods or beverages. The skins are likely to be coated with insecticides or other unwholesome matter.

☐ When substituting lemon juice for vinegar in a recipe, double the quantity called for.

LETTUCE

☐ Iceberg lettuce has its good and bad points. On the positive side, it has a comparatively long storage life and adds a desirable crispy texture to tacos and sandwiches. As a salad green, however, iceberg is too bland for discerning palates. Iceberg is also unsuitable because dressings don't readily cling to its smooth, slippery surfaces: Costly dressings end up in the bottom of the salad bowl.

☐ Excellent salad greens include Boston, Bibb, and romaine. For a pleasant bitter contrasting note, add greens, such as arugula and watercress.

☐ Whatever the type of lettuce you buy, the head should be well shaped and the color vivid. Wilting and bug holes are negative signs.

☐ Store lettuce sealed in a plastic bag in the vegetable crisper.

☐ Salad leaves must be dried after being washed so that the salad dressing clings to the leaves and doesn't become diluted.

☐ Unless you use a very sharp knife or you plan to eat the lettuce soon after cutting it into pieces, you should rip the

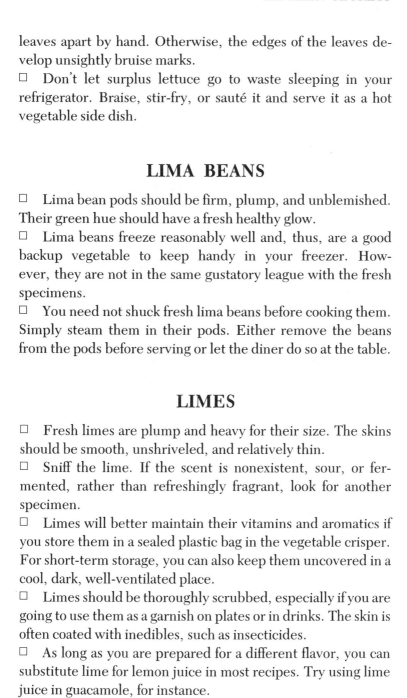

leaves apart by hand. Otherwise, the edges of the leaves develop unsightly bruise marks.

☐ Don't let surplus lettuce go to waste sleeping in your refrigerator. Braise, stir-fry, or sauté it and serve it as a hot vegetable side dish.

LIMA BEANS

☐ Lima bean pods should be firm, plump, and unblemished. Their green hue should have a fresh healthy glow.

☐ Lima beans freeze reasonably well and, thus, are a good backup vegetable to keep handy in your freezer. However, they are not in the same gustatory league with the fresh specimens.

☐ You need not shuck fresh lima beans before cooking them. Simply steam them in their pods. Either remove the beans from the pods before serving or let the diner do so at the table.

LIMES

☐ Fresh limes are plump and heavy for their size. The skins should be smooth, unshriveled, and relatively thin.

☐ Sniff the lime. If the scent is nonexistent, sour, or fermented, rather than refreshingly fragrant, look for another specimen.

☐ Limes will better maintain their vitamins and aromatics if you store them in a sealed plastic bag in the vegetable crisper. For short-term storage, you can also keep them uncovered in a cool, dark, well-ventilated place.

☐ Limes should be thoroughly scrubbed, especially if you are going to use them as a garnish on plates or in drinks. The skin is often coated with inedibles, such as insecticides.

☐ As long as you are prepared for a different flavor, you can substitute lime for lemon juice in most recipes. Try using lime juice in guacamole, for instance.

LIQUEURS AND SPIRITS

☐ The quickest and easiest way to heat liqueurs or spirits for flambéing is to place the quantity you need in a microwave oven set at high. Allow about 15 seconds per ounce.

☐ *See also* Flambéing.

LOBSTERS

Marketplace Pointers

☐ Make sure the lobster is still alive. If it's dead, pathogenic microorganisms contaminate the flesh within a few hours of its demise.

☐ Should you have doubts that the lobster is alive, pick it up. If its tail doesn't curl under its body, the lobster is dead (or practically dead).

☐ Gourmets prefer the female to the male lobster, because the female contains the esteemed coral-colored roe. Here's how to tell the female from the male. Turn the lobster over and look for a pair of tiny antennae-like protuberances located immediately behind the walking legs. If they are relatively soft, short, thin, and slightly feathery, you are holding a female.

☐ Unless the tail of a precooked lobster curls underneath its body, the lobster wasn't alive when the merchant began cooking it and, therefore, eating it is risky.

☐ Give the lobster the "sniff" test; it should smell fresh and have no off odor.

Kitchen Hints

☐ Before plunging a live lobster into a pot of boiling water, take this humane step that partially desensitizes the crustacean: Sever its spinal cord by plunging a knife an inch or two into the crevice between its body and tail sections.

☐ People tend to overcook lobsters and, therefore, end up with unnecessarily dry, tough, and shrunken meat. After you put the lobster in a pot of vigorously boiling water, simmer it for only 5 minutes plus 3 minutes for each pound.

☐ When broiling a split lobster, baste it often with butter to keep the flesh moist and tender. Use herb butter for a special flavor.

☐ Frozen lobster tails come from spiny lobsters rather than from the true lobster (*Homarus americanus*) and, thus, are not as sweet and tender. Should it be necessary for you to buy frozen lobster tails, be sure to let them thaw overnight in the refrigerator before you cook them. Otherwise, they will be very tough and dry.

LUNCH BOXES

☐ When packing a lunch box or brown bag, remember that bacteria thrive in the 40-to-140-degree range. Therefore, use efficient insulated containers to keep foods like cream soups hot and items like salami sandwiches cold.

☐ Freezer gel packs are ideal for keeping well-wrapped foods, such as sandwiches, cool in a lunch box. If your child is brown bagging it, consider freezing the sandwich overnight— it will thaw by lunchtime.

M

MACAROONS

☐ You double the storage life of your homemade macaroons when you wrap them individually in tissue or paper towels before placing them in an airtight container.

☐ Crumbled macaroons, sprinkled to top of ice cream, contribute both flavor and texture contrast.

MACE

☐ Blade (unground) mace is more aromatic and flavorful than the preground product. Add one or more of these pieces to soups and stews as they cook, but remember to discard them before serving.

☐ Preground mace, however, is a convenient spice to have in your kitchen. Adding a pinch to omelets or tuna salads, for instance, lends a new dimension in flavor.

☐ Keep a close eye and nose on your ground mace supply, as it can become rancid rather quickly.

MAIL ORDER

☐ Before ordering perishable goods from a mail-order house, verify that the firm will refund your money or replace the goods should the food arrive in poor condition.

☐ Should a gift that you sent through a mail-order house not arrive and the intended recipient doesn't know that it was supposed to arrive, you may never know of the nondelivery. It's a good idea to send the recipient a separate note, stating that he or she should expect a package on such and such a date.

☐ If a mail-order house bilks you, register a complaint with your local post office. Postal inspectors will investigate and take action on verifiable frauds. However, if you placed your order and paid for it by credit card on the phone, nonmail transactions are beyond their jurisdiction.

MANGOES

☐ Reject any mango that is green skinned and hard when squeezed: It will rot before it ripens.

☐ However, if the mango skin is mostly red or orange, and it yields slightly when squeezed, you can ripen it at home. Store it in a pierced paper bag at room temperature for one to several days.

☐ The skin of a ripe mango is yellow-orange to red with no traces of green. It has a pleasant aroma. If the skin is flecked with black spots or the fruit is soft or smells sour or fermented, the mango is overripe.

MAPLE SYRUP

☐ Buy pure, not maple-flavored, syrup because the difference in their flavors is significant. Maple-flavored syrup costs less, but it has less character, because the processor stretches the maple syrup with corn syrup. Even less desirable is "pancake syrup": It rarely contains one drop of maple syrup.

☐ Top-grade maple syrups should not necessarily be your first choice. If you enjoy the full flavor of maple syrup, opt for a lower grade. The top grades are usually too refined.

☐ Try substituting maple syrup for regular sugar as a sweetener in your hot cereals.

☐ Bring a refrigerated syrup to room temperature (or gently heat it) before serving it on top of your pancakes or waffles. Otherwise, the liquid will prematurely cool the food.

☐ Once opened, maple syrup should be refrigerated. Should

it develop crystals, set the syrup in a pan of hot water until the crystals disappear.

MARGARINE

☐   In terms of desirable flavor, margarine can never be a substitute for butter.

☐   The best margarines are made exclusively with poly-unsaturated safflower or corn oil. Mediocre margarines contain less expensive vegetable oils, such as cottonseed and coconut oils. Read the label.

☐   Stick margarine is better than soft margarine for sautéing and basting. Soft margarine, though, is easier to spread on bread.

☐   When comparing the cost between stick and soft margarine, take into consideration that soft margarine has a lot of air whipped into it. With some brands, the air comprises up to 50 percent of the total volume.

☐   Cholesterol watchers take note: Margarine (like butter) is well saturated with fat. Though it is true that the producers use unsaturated oils to make their products, these oils become saturated as a result of the manufacturing process.

☐   If you see the word "hydrogenated" in the ingredients list, you know for certain that the margarine contains saturated fats.

MARINATING

☐   By marinating food in a sealed plastic bag, you can reduce the amount of marinade you need. Turn the bag occasionally to coat the entire surface of the food. When finished, simply discard the bag.

☐   Don't reuse a marinade to marinate. It won't have sufficient acid to perform the marinating role, because the food you marinated likely contained alkali, a compound that neutralizes acid. Leftover marinade can be put to other culinary uses, such as flavoring a stew.

MASHED POTATOES

☐ For the best mashed potatoes, use Idaho or other russet potatoes rather than new potatoes.

☐ Combine only warm milk with mashed potatoes. Cold milk lowers the temperature of the potatoes and, thereby, makes them gummy.

☐ Mashed potatoes can also become gummy if you do not incorporate the milk gradually into the potatoes.

☐ The potatoes are cooked as soon as you can pierce their centers easily with the tip of a sharp paring knife.

☐ Whether you cook the potatoes peeled or not, properly drain them the moment they are cooked. Then, gently shake the potatoes in the pot for a half minute over low heat to dry their surfaces and rid them of excess moisture.

☐ If you overmash potatoes, you rupture their cell walls, allowing starch granules to escape. This produces gummy as opposed to light and airy mashed potatoes.

☐ Once the potatoes are mashed, don't cover the pot or bowl. Otherwise, the trapped steam will give the mashed potatoes a soggy consistency.

MEASURING

☐ You may misread the volume if you view the scale-markings of a glass measuring cup while looking over the rim. For accurate measuring, keep your eyes below the rim of the cup. In this way, light refraction won't create an optical illusion.

MEAT LOAF

☐ Meat loaf will be easier to slice if you let it rest for about 10 minutes after you remove it from the oven.

MEATS

☐ Meat shrinks as it roasts. If you want to minimize this costly loss, roast the meat at 275 degrees rather than at the customary 350-degree setting. Just increase the cooking time by one-third.

☐ Don't try to tenderize a steak by puncturing it with the tines of a fork. This tactic is counterproductive, because it creates channels for the internal juices of the meat to escape during the cooking process.

☐ If unexpected guests arrive for dinner, consider stretching your meat dish by cutting it into smaller pieces and serving it in a sauce over a bed of rice or pasta.

☐ *See also* Meat Thermometer, Commercial Meat Tenderizers, Pounding Meat, Beef, Lamb, Pork, and Veal.

MEAT THERMOMETER

☐ The probe of a meat thermometer should be placed in the thickest part of the meat away from any bone or fat. Should it come into contact with a bone, the reading will be erroneously high, because bone is a good conductor of heat. If the probe touches fat, the reverse occurs as fat is a poor heat conductor.

MELONS

Marketplace Pointers

☐ Examine the stem end of the melon. If the stem "crater" has jagged protuberances, the melon was harvested before it was mature and, therefore, will never reach succulent perfection.

☐ Avoid melons with shriveled skins, soft or discolored spots, and musty odors.

☐ All melons should be heavy for their size and type. Lightness indicates internal dehydration.

☐ A melon is overripe if it is soft when you squeeze it with the palms of your hands.

☐ Sniff the blossom end of the melon. If the fruit is ready to eat, you should be able to smell an inviting fragrance. One exception is the casaba which remains odorless. The melon is overripe if the fragrance is intense or hints of fermentation.

☐ A cantaloupe is immature if its natural surface netting doesn't stand out in relief from the underlying skin.

☐ If a honeydew melon is mature, its skin should have a modicum of texture and a yellowish or creamy white tone.

☐ With honeydews, "the bigger, the better" rule holds true. The early or late season runts leave much to be desired.

Kitchen Hints

☐ If you buy a slightly unripe melon, you can bring it to its full glory by storing it in a pierced paper bag in a cool, dry place for two to seven days, depending on the variety, size, and original degree of ripeness.

☐ If you discover that the melon you've opened is slightly unripe and, thereby, lacks flavor, turn it into melon balls. Then, marinate it in orange juice for at least several hours. Serve the two ingredients together in a small serving bowl.

☐ Once ripe, a melon decays quickly. Enjoy it at its peak. If you must delay opening it, seal it in a plastic bag and store it in the warmest part of the refrigerator.

☐ Save and pickle watermelon rinds. After paring off its green skin and pink interior, cut it into approximately 1-inch cubes and refrigerate them overnight in a sweet (sugared) pickling mixture.

☐ The flavor nuances of quality melons are best savored at room temperature or, at least, no colder than 50 degrees. Lower temperatures numb your taste buds.

☐ Leftover opened melon should be sealed in plastic wrap, refrigerated, and consumed as soon as possible. Prolonged storage robs the flesh of its scent, taste, and texture.

☐   If you plan to store an opened melon for more than a day, don't scoop out the seeds. Their moisture helps to keep the flesh from drying out.

☐   *See also* Watermelon.

MICROWAVE COOKING

☐   Reheating food in a lead crystal dish is inadvisable. The metal in the glass will reflect the microwaves, slowing down the cooking process and possibly damaging the oven.

☐   Food will cook more uniformly in a round, rather than a square or rectangular, pan.

☐   Be cautious about microwaving food in a tightly sealed container, such as a plastic tub. Unless built-up steam can escape, an explosion might take place.

☐   Be wary when you microwave certain foods, such as whole unpierced potatoes, tomatoes, egg yolks, plantains, or zucchini. Explosions are possible because of their relatively impervious skins and membranes.

☐   Food generally cooks faster near the sides than in the center of a microwave oven. Therefore, when cooking an irregularly shaped piece of food, such as a chicken leg, place the thickest portion nearest the oven walls.

☐   To determine the hottest and coldest cooking spots in your oven, completely carpet the oven floor with a layer of trimmed, untoasted bread slices. Set the oven on high and observe the browning process through the glass door. Stop the experiment before any of the toast burns.

MILK

Marketplace Pointers

☐   Given a choice, buy your milk in bottles. Plastic and especially wax-coated cartons can give milk an off flavor.

☐   If your bottled milk is delivered to your doorstep, be sure it never sits in direct sunlight. Solar rays destroy flavor and nutrients.

☐   Otherwise identical cartons of milk in a store could differ in age. Always look for the latest date.

☐   Milk provides children with calcium for their young bones. If you buy chocolate milk, however, this benefit is partially negated, because chocolate hinders the digestion of calcium.

Kitchen Hints

☐   Reconstituted milk powder will be less grainy and have less of a baked flavor if you prepare it a day ahead of time.

☐   Milk in a wax-coated carton will absorb odors from other refrigerated foods if the spout is not tightly closed. Consider sealing the spout with a clip, such as a small clothes pin.

☐   If the recipe calls for whole milk, and you have only skim milk on hand, you can substitute 1 cup of skim milk plus 2 teaspoons of melted unsalted butter for each cup of whole milk needed.

☐   Scalding milk for a recipe is unnecessary if your milk is pasteurized. Such milk has already been heated to a high enough temperature during the pasteurization process to denature the enzymes that could otherwise hinder, for example, the thickening of a sauce.

MINT

☐   Fresh mint deserves to be used more often than it is. Mint has a special affinity to vegetables, such as peas, carrots, eggplant, cauliflower, and zucchini. This herb also adds a fillip to green and fresh fruit salads, as well as to sautéed chicken dishes and, of course, roast lamb.

MINT JELLY

◻ One of the most fatuous culinary traditions is serving lamb with mint jelly. The assertively minty and cloying flavor of that condiment overwhelms the lamb.

MOLASSES

◻ Of the three basic types of molasses, the cook's choices should be the light and dark varieties. The glories of the third, blackstrap molasses, have been overglamorized. It has a bitter flavor and contains indigestible byproducts.

MORTAR AND PESTLE

◻ Marble pestles are superior to wooden ones. You can exert firm pressure when grinding, because marble is more durable and won't crack or warp when wet. Marble won't absorb the scents of foods, such as garlic, transferring them to the next batch of food.
◻ The bowl should be sufficiently deep so that the ingredients don't fly over the sides while you are mashing them.

MSG

◻ Monosodium glutamate (MSG) gives cooked foods a curious off flavor, which partially explains why few good cooks use it.

MUSHROOMS

Marketplace Pointers

◻ It's better to hand select your mushrooms out of a bin rather than buying the prepackaged variety. Though loose mushrooms are more expensive, they are usually of high quality and are less likely to have been sprayed with the chemical preservative, sodium bisulfite. Moreover, you won't end up with wastage because you buy only the quantity you require for short-term consumption.

☐ The standard whole white mushroom is no longer in prime condition when the rim of its cap separates from the stem, exposing the gills under the cap.

☐ The surface of a standard mushroom can be white or slightly brown-flecked. However, if the flecking is excessive, or if there are any bruises or soft spots, the mushroom isn't worth buying.

☐ Because the cap is more tender and decorative than the stem, select mushrooms that have relatively short stems for their size.

☐ Buy even-sized mushrooms for the sake of even cooking and, should you slice them, a uniform look.

☐ Fresh mushrooms are so plentiful and easy to prepare that frozen or canned mushrooms should be out of the question for any serious cook.

Kitchen Hints

☐ Don't store mushrooms in a closed container or a sealed bag; they need a generous supply of cool, moist air to stay fresh. One effective storage method is to wrap the mushrooms loosely with slightly damp paper towels and store the package in the vegetable crisper.

☐ Don't toss out your mushrooms if they have deteriorated to the point of losing their visual appeal. As long as they are still reasonably fresh, you can chop them for use as a flavoring agent for preparations such as sauces and stews.

☐ Mushrooms soak up a lot of water greedily and, therefore, should not be washed in water if you plan to sauté them. Instead, gently wipe away their surface dirt and any chemical preservatives with a small damp cloth or paper towel.

HOWARD HILLMAN

☐   If you are not a knife pro, try slicing a whole mushroom in an egg slicer, cap side down.

☐   For a simple but decorative touch, cut whole mushrooms into "ionic columns" by quartering the whole mushrooms vertically.

☐   The cut flesh of raw mushrooms darkens quickly. Prepare them at the last minute or coat their exposed surfaces with lemon juice or another acidic liquid.

☐   Stuff fresh mushroom caps with blue cheese that has been lightly mashed with walnut or olive oil. Garnish with a ¼-inch-square piece of roasted sweet red pepper.

☐   Your mushrooms will be more flavorful and have a better texture if you sauté them in butter before adding them to a stew or braised dish.

☐   Sautéed mushrooms must be sautéed, not steam-sautéed. Steam-sautéing occurs when too many mushrooms are cooked in the pan at the same time. In this case, the trapped steam under the cooking mushrooms cannot escape into the air. Steam-sautéing can also take place if the cook uses mushrooms that were soaked in water.

MUSHROOMS (DRIED)

☐   Store dried mushrooms in a tightly closed jar in a cool, dark place. For optimum flavor, they should be used within several months.

☐   Dried mushrooms should be washed and soaked prior to use even if you are adding them to a soup or stew. Reason: Grit often lurks inside their folds. Strain the soaking water and use it as a flavoring agent.

MUSSELS

Marketplace Pointers

☐   For optimum tenderness, select the smallest mussels of a given variety.

☐ For even cooking, choose even-sized specimens.

☐ One bad mussel can spoil a whole dish. Therefore, keep these criteria in mind: Mussels that are heavy for their size may be full of sand. Those that are light for their size are probably dead or dying. Those that do not close when they are tapped and those with broken shells are also inedible or, at best, unsavory.

Kitchen Hints

☐ If you soak mussels in cool water for at least 2 hours, they will expel internal sand and waste.

☐ Never eat mussels raw. Some are typhoid fever carriers. Note: Proper cooking eliminates the typhoid fever threat.

☐ Before cooking, scrub mussels well and pull out their beards, a hairlike growth.

☐ When steaming unshucked mussels, simmer (do not boil) the liquid. Don't lift the lid for at least 5 minutes. Overcooking toughens their tender flesh.

MUSTARD

☐ Instead of buying flavored mustards, buy the plain variety and season a portion of it to suit the dish or sandwich you are preparing.

☐ In many homes, mustard is an overlooked ingredient for flavoring salad dressings and cooked dishes, such as stews. Naturally, use a quality mustard.

☐ If your consumption of mustard is low and you have an oversized crock of mustard, transfer part of this condiment to a smaller serving container, refilling it as needed. Keep the crock tightly covered and refrigerated. Your mustard supply will stay fresh longer because you will have minimized the number of times the mustard is exposed to the air.

☐ *See also* Condiments.

HOWARD HILLMAN

MUSTARD GREENS

☐ If too mature, mustard greens will have developed an undesirable, assertive flavor and fibrous midribs. Buy young specimens.

N

NECTARINES

☐ Nectarines are first cousins to the peach. All the tips given for peaches are equally valid.
☐ *See also* Peaches.

NUTMEG

☐ Whole nutmeg is sold in two forms: plain or dusted with a white powder. Given a choice, buy the unadulterated nutmeg.
☐ Why any serious cook should buy commercial, preground nutmeg has always escaped me. The freshly ground whole nutmeg is so much more aromatic. Moreover, the handheld metal nutmeg graters are easy to use, commonly available, and inexpensive.
☐ Some cooks grate only the outer portion of the nutmeg. For the record, the entire nutmeg is usable.

NUTS

Marketplace Pointers

☐ When buying unshelled nuts, look for those that are heavy for their size and uniform in hue and dimensions. The shells should be clean and unblemished and free of mold, cracks, and worm holes.
☐ Shake an unshelled nut. With the exception of a peanut, a nut is not fresh if it rattles.
☐ If you see more than a small amount of fine particles at the bottom of the jar or cellophane bag, the nuts are probably not fresh.

HOWARD HILLMAN

☐　Nuts become stale and rancid much quicker in a cellophane bag than in a jar or can.

☐　Before buying a bag of shelled nuts, snap one of the nuts in two in the package. Unless this nut snaps crisply, the entire contents of the bag is probably rancid.

☐　Try to sniff the nuts through the cellophane wrapper, too. Don't buy them if you detect the slightest rancid odor.

Kitchen Hints

☐　To help prevent rancidity, store your shelled nuts in a covered jar in the refrigerator. Refrigerate unshelled nuts in a plastic bag.

☐　Having a difficult time cracking pecans, almonds, and other hand-shelled nuts? Pour them into a pot of boiling water and turn off the heat. Remove the pecans in 10 minutes, the almonds in 2 minutes. Start cracking the nuts.

☐　Shelled nuts are easier to chop or sliver if they are heated for 5 minutes in a 350-degree oven.

☐　Food processors are good for turning shelled nuts into a paste, but not for chopping them.

☐　To improve the flavor of nuts purchased in jars and cans, roast them in a preheated 375-degree oven for approximately 5 to 10 minutes before serving them.

☐　The Soviet Georgians frequently use ground walnuts and West Africans, ground peanuts, to add body and flavor to their sauces and stews.

O

OILS

☐ Oil is best purchased in a can because damaging light rays easily pass through clear glass bottles. Once opened, however, the oil will develop a pronounced metallic flavor as a result of the oxygen reacting to the metal. For this reason, the exposed oil should be transferred to a glass bottle or jar with a tight-fitting lid.

☐ Cooking oils become rancid quickly. Buy for short-term consumption.

☐ If you do buy a large container for the sake of economy, transfer its contents to small bottles once it is opened. These bottles should be filled to maximum capacity (air causes rancidity) and stored in a cool, dark place.

☐ Unless you use a partially filled container of olive oil within a couple of weeks, refrigerate it. It will cloud or even solidify, but those conditions will disappear once you bring the oil to room temperature.

☐ *See also* Olive Oil, Sesame Oil, and Walnut Oil.

OKRA

☐ Buy small (young) okra with vivid green skins and firm, yet slightly flexible, pods. Blemishes and flaccidness are negative indicators.

☐ Okra is a natural thickener for stews. However, if you overcook this vegetable, it will develop a slimy texture.

☐ Okra will thicken a stew faster if you cook it cut up rather than whole. Since okra cooks much faster in a cut-up state, watch the pot closely.

HOWARD HILLMAN

OLIVE OIL

☐ For salad dressing, buy the milder, more subtley flavored olive oils, such as those produced in Lucca, Italy. For sautéing hearty dishes, the more robust and flavorful olive oils, such as those from Sicily are generally preferred.

☐ Whether you are buying a subtle or robust style olive oil, the virgin variety should be your first choice. It is lightly pressed, relatively low in acid, and additive free.

☐ If the olive oil is not classified as "virgin," be sure it, at least, merits the "pure" designation. Blended olive oils are stretched with less expensive oils.

☐ *See also* Gifts.

OLIVES

☐ Keeping olives in their opened can will appreciably curtail their storage life. Transfer them, with their brine, to a glass or plastic container. Cover and refrigerate.

☐ If you want to prolong the storage life of olives you've purchased out of the tub or barrel, put them in a glass or plastic container and add a little olive oil to coat the fruit. Cover, refrigerate, and use within a week.

ONIONS

Marketplace Pointers

☐ Dehydrated onions in any form—flakes, powdered, whatever—are gastronomic insults. Fresh onions are so readily available, relatively inexpensive, and easy to prepare that there should be no excuse for substituting unsavory dehydrated onion products for them.

☐ Equally detestable are frozen onion products, such as chopped onions. Because they have lost so much of their flavor and texture and have developed new off-putting flavors, any gain in convenience is nullified.

☐   For most culinary applications, the white-skinned (silver-skin) onion is preferable to the larger, yellow-skinned onion, because it isn't as sweet and has a sharper, more pronounced flavor that will stand up to the cooking process. The standard yellow-skinned onion, however, is less expensive and is "de rigueur" for certain specialties, such as onion soup and french fried onion rings. For the above reasons, a well-stocked kitchen will have both white and yellow onions on hand.

☐   The purple-skinned Bermuda onion is a good choice for eating raw in salads and sandwiches, because of its relatively mild flavor.

☐   Pearl onions are excellent choices for stews and creamed dishes. Peel and cook them whole.

☐   Onions should be symmetrical and feel heavy for their size. Their skins should be dry, shiny, and unblemished, without green-tinted sunburn marks.

☐   Squeeze the onion. It should be firm, without soft spots. Examine the neck: It should be small, firm, and tightly closed without any evidence of sprouting.

☐   Packaged onions cost less per pound than the loose variety, but they are seldom values, because they usually are sprouting or rotting by the time you get around to using all of them.

Kitchen Hints

☐   Unless you are going to use your onions within a day or two of purchase, they should be stored in a basket or wide, un-covered bowl in a cool, dry, dark, well-ventilated spot. Under no circumstances should they be refrigerated, stored near the stove, or be exposed to sunlight.

☐   Keep track of your onion inventory. If you replenish your supply, use up the onions you purchased earlier first.

☐   The skins of some onion varieties are difficult to peel off quickly and neatly. Your task will be easier if you parboil these onions for a minute or two (depending on their size) and then quickly plunge them into cold water.

☐ If your eyes tear while you are cutting onions, wear safety goggles (sold in hardware stores), which will keep most of the volatile fumes from reaching your eyes.

☐ The sharper the knife, the less likely that tears will well up in your eyes.

☐ Promptly wash and dry a carbon steel knife after you cut onions; otherwise, the blade will discolor. A better idea is to cut onions with a stainless steel or other non-corrosive knife.

☐ Try not to prepare ahead of time more onions than you will need. Once cut open, they quickly lose their desirable flavor and develop objectionable qualities.

☐ If you have leftover chopped onions, store them in a glass jar (never in a plastic container, as it readily absorbs onion odor).

☐ If you have a leftover onion half, wrap it tightly in plastic wrap and refrigerate. If possible, don't remove its skin.

☐ To keep the core of a whole onion from popping out as it cooks, cut a ⅛- to ¼-inch-deep "X" pattern on its root end.

☐ Onions develop a harsh flavor if they are sautéed too long or over too high a heat. For best results, sauté them for no more than several minutes over moderate heat. As soon as they become soft and translucent, lower the cooking temperature by adding—for instance—wine to the pan.

☐ For the sake of flavor and shape, whole "boiled onions" should be simmered, never boiled.

☐ For optimum whiteness, onions should be young, fresh, and not overcooked. Adding an acidic ingredient such as lemon juice or cream of tartar also helps keep the onions from turning yellow.

ORANGE JUICE

☐ When buying frozen orange juice, be sure the package is frozen solid and there is no sticky leakage.

☐   Orange juice made from the frozen concentrated product will taste better if you reconstitute it at least 12 hours ahead of time.

ORANGES

☐   For orange juice, your best bets are usually the thin-skinned Florida oranges. Besides being juicy, these oranges make a pleasant drink, because they contain enough acid to balance out their sweetness.

☐   For eating out of the hand, the thick-skinned California navel oranges are normally your best bet.

☐   Whatever the variety of orange that you buy, select ones that are relatively heavy for their size. These oranges will be juicier than their lighter bin mates.

☐   A ripe and mature orange usually is, as its name suggests, orange. However, a green tinge on a Florida juice orange does not necessarily indicate unripeness. Oranges from sub-tropical and, especially tropical climes, are often green when ripe. (Note: A Florida orange may be green-tinged without you knowing it because the state allows the processor to dye the rind orange.)

☐   Oranges should be firm, not soft or spongy. You should see no evidence of mold, cuts, or blemishes.

☐   Sniff the orange. If you smell even the slightest hint of fermentation, the orange has seen fresher days.

☐   Oranges prepackaged in netted bags are not the value they seem at first glance. Chances are some of the oranges will be of inferior quality. And, if there is one spoiled orange in the bag, it could hasten the deterioration of the other oranges.

☐   To preserve the vitamin C content of oranges, store the oranges in a sealed plastic bag in the refrigerator. For periods longer than several days, however, the bag should be slightly open to allow the fruit to breathe.

☐   Plan on buying 2 medium-sized oranges for each ½ cup (4-ounce) serving of juice. If the oranges are especially juicy, they will yield 5 ounces.

OREGANO

☐   The character of oregano varies considerably according to its variety and origin. Paying a premium for quality as opposed to "pizza parlor grade" oregano is a good culinary investment.

OVENS

☐   Before buying a restaurant-style oven for your home, be sure you have sufficient ventilation, because these commercial units generate considerable fumes and heat. The heat may even scorch adjacent wood walls and shelves.

☐   Most home ovens give a false temperature reading, usually off by as much as 25 degrees in either direction, enough to cause a recipe failure. Test your oven's temperature gauge against a reliable oven thermometer (buy one or borrow one from a friend) at least twice a year. Make temperature tests at 250, 350, and 450 degrees. Then make mental adjustments accordingly (for instance, if your oven reads 375 degrees when its dial says 350 degrees, set the oven at 300 degrees when the recipe calls for 325 degrees).

☐   If you're using the heat of the oven pilot light to defrost vegetables or warm plates, drop a colorful fire resistant ribbon over the oven door handle as a "don't turn on the oven" reminder.

OXTAILS

☐   Freshly butchered oxtails have a vivid red hue and a clean scent.

☐   Oxtails need to be cooked by a slow, moist method, such as braising or simmering.

☐   The older the animal, the longer the oxtail segments need to be cooked.

OYSTERS

Marketplace Pointers

☐   The smaller the oyster for its variety, the more tender it will be. However, selecting the smallest oysters in the lot has its disadvantages. You'll have to work harder to open a given weight.

☐   To estimate age, look at the concentric shell rings; like tree rings, each pronounced ridge represents one year of age.

☐   Do not necessarily equate the size of the oyster shell with the size of its meat. Before buying a batch, ask the seller to open one.

☐   Avoid oysters that feel heavy or light for their size: The first may contain sand; the second may be dead.

☐   Don't buy oysters with broken shells. Ditto for oysters that refuse to close tightly when tapped. (They are dead or on their way.)

☐   If your recipe calls for cooking the oysters, buy even-sized specimens. They'll cook evenly.

Kitchen Hints

☐   An oyster has a shallow and deep half shell. Your oyster will stay fresh longer if you store it resting on the larger shell half.

☐   Before you shuck an oyster, let it rest in peace and quiet. Such an oyster will resist shucking less than an agitated one.

☐   Another way to relax an oyster is to place it in the freezer for about 10 minutes, but not longer lest the freezing process toughen the flesh.

☐   Don't try to open an oyster with a clam knife, which has a round tip. You'll need an oyster knife, one with a sharper, more angular tip.

P

PANCAKES

☐ A pancake will toughen if it is turned more than once.

☐ Turn a pancake when the bubbles that have developed on its surface begin to pop. Fry the second side for roughly half the time required for the first.

PANCAKE SYRUP

☐ The cap of a syrup tin or bottle will be easier to open if you make it a habit to wipe the cap and the grooved neck of the container after each meal.

☐ Out of pancake syrup? Mix and gently heat three parts jam, one part unsalted butter, and one part water. Spoon the warm mixture over your pancakes.

PAN-FRYING

☐ If a steak or chop has a rim of fat, slash it at 1-inch intervals. This prevents the meat from curling and, therefore, from cooking unevenly.

☐ It's time to turn beef when blood droplets begin appearing on the top (uncooked) surface of the steak or patty.

PAPAYAS

☐ The common papaya is not ripe until its green skin turns completely yellow and the fruit emits its characteristic sweet fruity fragrance.

☐ Gently squeeze the papaya. If the fruit is too firm or too soft, don't buy it.

☐ Slightly unripe papayas can be brought to eating condition by storing them in a pierced paper bag at room temperature for no more than a few days.

☐ A natural affinity: several drops of lime juice rubbed on a papaya slice.

PAPRIKA

☐ Ask the merchant for the country of origin. The Hungarian-grown paprika is of higher quality than the more commonly available Spanish variety.

☐ Hungarian paprika comes in three levels of hotness: mild (also called "sweet"), hot, and exceptionally hot. Most of the paprika sold in this country is the mild version and is the preferred choice for flavoring dishes such as chicken paprika. It is also widely used for sprinkling on top of foods to add color.

PARSLEY

☐ The two basic types of fresh parsley are the flat leaf Italian and the curly leaf varieties. The first has a more enticing flavor and, therefore, should be your first choice for cooking. Curly leaf parsley, however, makes a more attractive garnish.

☐ Why buy dried or freeze-dried parsley when the infinitely superior fresh parsley is relatively inexpensive and is readily available in the market place?

☐ You can store your fresh parsley for up to two weeks by placing it root end down in a tall canning jar that has a rubber sealing ring. Add 1 inch of water, close the jar and refrigerate. Change the water every other day. If you don't have a suitable canning jar, substitute a regular jar. Cover the top of the herb with a plastic bag fastened to the lidless jar with a rubber band.

PARSNIPS

☐ Buy small-to-medium-sized parsnips. Mature ones have a dry, fibrous texture and lack delicate flavor.

☐ Parsnips will retain more of their natural sweet flavor and be more nutritious if you cook them unpeeled.

☐ Overcooked parsnips become mushy and undesirable. Add them to a stew toward the end of the cooking period.

PASTA

Marketplace Pointers

☐ Scrutinize the package. If the box or cellophane envelope is not sealed tightly, the pasta may have suffered oxidation or pest damage.

☐ The pasta inside the package should be whole, not broken. If you see more than a smidgen of powder in the package, the pasta has probably been stored improperly or for too long.

☐ Freshly made pasta is preferable, in most instances, to dried pasta. However, when comparing the price per pound between dried and freshly made pasta, remember that the weight of the latter is mostly water when you buy it. (Dry pasta regains its moisture when you cook it.)

☐ If serving a thick pasta sauce, you would probably be better off buying dried pasta rather than freshly made pasta. The firmer the texture of the pasta, the more likely the sauce will cling.

☐ Quality brand pastas are preferable to less expensive ones, because they are tastier and have a better texture. They also have a less starchy exterior, which can cause pasta pieces to stick together after they are cooked and drained.

☐ When planning to mix white and green pasta, don't purchase the two types on a one-to-one ratio. A three-to-one, white-to-green ratio makes a more attractive presentation.

Kitchen Hints

☐   Once its package is opened, pasta can quickly become stale or rancid (due to oxidation) or be attacked by bugs. Therefore, store an opened box of pasta in a sealed plastic bag in a cool, dark place. Or, better yet, transfer the contents to an airtight glass or plastic container.

☐   Whole wheat pasta becomes rancid quickly. If you can, plan to use it within a week of purchase. Store it in the refrigerator, but bring it to room temperature before cooking it.

☐   Pasta will be less likely to stick together if you add a small amount of oil (preferably olive oil) to the water before you add the pasta.

☐   The water should be vigorously boiling before you put in the pasta. The water to pasta ratio should be sufficiently high (at least 1 quart of water per pound of pasta) so that the water temperature doesn't appreciably drop when you add the pasta.

☐   When cooking long strands of pasta, don't break them to fit into the pot. Ease them gradually into the water as they bend and soften.

☐   Unlike dried pasta, freshly made pasta needs to be boiled for only 1 or 2 minutes. Further cooking destroys texture and causes gumminess.

☐   To test dried or freshly made pasta for doneness, remove a sample from the water. Make a cross-sectional cut at its thickest point. When the white chalkiness in the interior is reduced to a point or hairline, immediately drain and serve the pasta. (Since the pasta continues to cook after you drain it, the remaining chalkiness will have disappeared by the time the diner takes his first bite.)

☐   Some recipes recommend that you rinse the cooked pasta under cold water to keep the pieces from sticking together. This step is counterproductive because it cools the pasta, making it a less steaming treat at the dinner table.

☐   However, when making a cold preparation, such as a cold

pasta salad, briefly rinse the just-cooked pasta, under cold running water.

□   If the cooked pasta has stuck together after it has left the pan, mix in a little of the hot cooking water. Alternatively, place the cooked pasta in boiling water containing 1 tablespoon of oil for each cup of water. Stir the pasta gently for 1 minute and then drain it.

□   Pasta should be served in a warm bowl and on warm plates.

□   Consider mixing the pasta and its sauce at the table, not in the kitchen. Spoon the sauce on top of the pasta in the center of the bowl without mixing the ingredients. Better yet, serve the pasta and its sauce separately. Let each diner spoon the sauce over his served portion according to taste. Pasta presented unmixed is more aesthetically pleasing and doesn't get soggy prematurely.

PASTRAMI

□   Because it is made from the plate or brisket, both tough cuts of meat, pastrami needs to be sliced against the grain.

□   For a juicier pastrami, choose meat from the plate rather than from the brisket primal.

□   When reheating a chunk of pastrami, steam it. Dry heat makes the meat chewy.

PASTRY

□   Quality suffers significantly if you substitute oil for part of the butter in a pastry recipe. Butter gives pastry a desirable light texture as well as flavor.

□   When making pastry dough, keep the butter cool or the dough won't expand to its full potential in the oven. Work in a cool kitchen and handle the dough as little as possible.

□   The butter will stay cold longer if you chill the pastry board and roller beforehand in your refrigerator or freezer.

☐ Because they stay cool, marble slabs are ideal for making butter-rich pastry doughs.

☐ If the dough begins to develop a greasy sheen, you know that the butter is beginning to melt. Wrap the dough in plastic wrap or place it in a covered bowl, then refrigerate the dough for 20 to 30 minutes before proceeding with the recipe.

☐ Pastries made with a high egg content should be refrigerated if they are not to be eaten within a few hours after coming out of the oven. For the sake of flavor, bring a refrigerated pastry to room temperature before serving it.

PÂTÉS AND TERRINES

☐ The fat surrounding the meat in a terrine is not meant to be eaten. The primary function of this gastronomically dull layer of fat is to keep the meat from drying out during the cooking process.

☐ The flavor of a homemade pâté or terrine will be more invitingly complex if you refrigerate it at least a day or two before serving it. Just be sure to bring it to room temperature before serving it.

PEACHES

☐ Frozen or canned peaches always have deplorable textures and flavors. Fresh peaches do or don't, depending largely on the peaches' degree of ripeness.

☐ The surest test for ripeness is to sniff the peach. If it isn't enticingly fragrant, it's not ripe.

☐ Nor is the peach ripe if it is rock hard or green tinged.

☐ Round peaches have better flavor profiles than flattened ones.

☐ Avoid peaches that have blemishes, soft spots, worm holes, sticky leaks, or shriveled skins.

☐ Don't let the check-out clerk treat your peaches carelessly. They bruise easily and the damaged areas will rot quickly.

☐ If the peach is hard to begin with, it will rot before it ripens. However, if it is almost ripe, you can finish the ripening process successfully at home by storing the peach in a pierced paper bag at room temperature for a day or two.

☐ Once ripe, eat peaches promptly or store them in a sealed plastic bag in the vegetable crisper for up to a couple of days.

☐ Peel peaches before using them in pies, jams, and other cooked preparations. Otherwise, their skins will shrivel into unchewable morsels, diminishing the diner's pleasure.

☐ Once peeled, peaches will start to turn brown unless you cook them or coat their exposed flesh with sugar or an acidic ingredient, such as lemon juice.

PEANUT BUTTER

☐ If you have the option, buy freshly made peanut butter and in small quantities. Though it has a much shorter storage life, the freshly ground product has a more rewarding flavor than the preprocessed supermarket variety.

☐ Don't worry if some of the oil separates from your freshly made peanut butter. That is bound to happen, because this spread contains no stabilizers, as do the national brands. Simply stir the oil back into the peanut butter before using it.

☐ Once opened, peanut butter will stay fresh longer if you refrigerate rather than store it at room temperature.

☐ Save your wide-mouthed peanut butter jars for storing soups and stocks in the frozen food compartment. Because these jars have wide openings, you can transfer the food quickly from the container to a pot without having to wait for the contents to thaw.

PEANUTS

☐ Dieters, take note: Dry-roasted peanuts and regular roasted peanuts have about the same caloric content.

PEARS

☐ Most pears are picked long before they are mature and, hence, tend to be dry, coarse textured, and relatively bland rather than juicy, soft textured, and spicy sweet.

☐ Select pears that are firm yet slightly resistent when squeezed. Reject rock-hard pears: They'll rot before they ever ripen. Don't buy soft pears: They have probably partially deteriorated.

☐ If you can't smell the pear's characteristic aroma through its skin, the fruit is not worth buying.

☐ The pear's skin should be free of blemishes, cracking, and soft spots.

☐ To bring an almost ripe pear to eating condition, store it in a pierced paper bag at room temperature for a day or two.

☐ Once they have ripened, pears deteriorate rapidly. Either eat them promptly or store them in a sealed plastic bag in the vegetable crisper for up to a couple of days.

☐ Canned pears are too mushy and curiously flavored to be taken seriously by true pear lovers.

☐ The exposed flesh of pears turns brown quickly. Eat, cook, or coat the surface with lemon juice or other acidic liquid soon after you cut the fruit.

☐ Pears lack the acidity of apples and, therefore, usually benefit from the companionship of an acidic ingredient when cooked. This partially explains why pears poached in wine is a classic dessert.

PEAS

☐ Here's how to buy peas in the pod: Look for pods that are small (indicating youth), firm yet flexible, and vivid green; the peas inside should be fresh and reasonably uniform in size (open a sample).

☐ When in doubt about the quality of a batch of shelled peas, cover them with water in a bowl. Discard those that float.

☐ If fresh peas are not obtainable, don't shy away from frozen peas. Unlike most vegetables, peas freeze reasonably well.

☐ Generally, baby peas are preferable to the standard-sized ones in terms of delicate flavor.

☐ Don't cook peas covered if you are preparing them with acidic ingredients, such as lemon juice or tomatoes. Otherwise, they can easily develop an unwanted olive-drab hue, especially if they are overcooked to even the slightest degree.

PEPPERCORNS

☐ Anyone who uses preground peppercorns in the kitchen or the dining room has probably never cross-tested the aromas of preground and the peppermill-ground types. The latter gives the diner more pleasure.

☐ Some peppercorn varieties have more enticing aromas and flavors than do others. Tellicherry from India is generally considered to be the world's finest.

☐ White peppercorns have one culinary value: The ground ingredient won't be visible in a light-colored sauce. For all other preparations, black peppercorns are preferable, because they have a richer, more aromatic character.

PEPPERMILLS

☐ For the sake of variety, why not have more than one peppermill for grinding different types of peppercorns?

☐ Inexpensive peppermills usually prove to be poor values in the long run. A well-made peppermill should last many years.

PERSIMMONS

☐ Look for persimmons that still have their stem and caps, which should be green and pliable.

☐ The skin should be free of blemishes, cracks, and bruises. Soft spots are rot spots.

☐ Unfortunately, a reddish-orange color is no longer a reliable indicator of maturity and ripeness. Many persimmons are treated with ethylene gas, a process that artificially turns their skins from green to reddish-orange.

☐ Persimmons usually must be ripened at home, because nearly all the specimens displayed at the greengrocer have not yet lost their astringent flavor. Should you find a ripe persimmon, it is probably well bruised due to frequent handling by previous shoppers.

☐ Ripen a persimmon in a sealed paper bag at room temperature until the fruit feels slightly soft when lightly squeezed. In most instances, the ripening process will take several days.

☐ Eat the persimmon as soon as it ripens. A delay results in a fruit with a mushy texture.

☐ The skin is edible if you wash the fruit thoroughly to rid it of possible insecticides.

☐ If you are cooking with persimmons, remove the skin unless you are cooking the fruit whole. Don't overcook the persimmons or they will become bitter.

PICKLES

☐ Look for pickles that are small for their variety. They'll be less seedy, mushy, and bitter than their larger brothers.

☐ When buying pickles out of a barrel, select those with a fresh green hue. As they sit around waiting to be purchased, their surfaces gradually acquire a pale, grayish tint.

☐ If the pickle is fresh, you should feel and hear it snap when you bite into it.

PICKLING

☐ For better flavor, texture, and color, use non-iodized salt for pickling cucumbers and other foods.

148

HOWARD HILLMAN

PICNICS

☐ When selecting your wardrobe for a picnic, remember that light-colored clothes keep you cooler on a hot sunny day and that dark-colored clothes are more apt to make bees aggressive.

☐ Insulated containers will keep food colder longer if you store them overnight in the freezer before using them.

PIE DOUGH

☐ For a crusty pie dough, use fat (lard, butter, etc.) rather than vegetable oil as the shortening. Also, don't overcut the fat into the flour; stop as soon as the texture reaches the coarse cornmeal stage.

☐ Save your leftover pie dough scraps. Make cookies out of them.

Pies. *See* Baking

PIGS' FEET

☐ The odor and flavor of pigs' feet noticeably increases in direct proportion to the age of the animal. If the scent of the pigs' feet you purchase is too assertive, parboil the trotters for about 15 minutes. Drain and then proceed with your recipe, cutting its suggested cooking time by 15 minutes.

PINEAPPLES

Marketplace Pointers

☐ Sniff the fruit. Unless it smells sweet, it won't taste sweet.
☐ Hold the pineapple in the palms of your hands and press it gently. It should feel firm yet springy.

□ Pineapples that are large for their variety have the most edible flesh per unit of weight.

□ The fruit should also be heavy for its size, indicating juiciness.

□ Examine the skin. Most pineapple varieties are ripe and mature when the skin hue is a lively golden orange or yellow. All traces of green should be gone. The pips should be plump, standing out in bold relief from the cross-hatching.

□ If you see mold or decay on the base of the pineapple, the odds are better than fifty-fifty that the interior pulp has started to deteriorate.

□ Examine the crown leaves. They should be small for the pineapple variety and, if the fruit is fresh, the leaves should be a bright, deep green without any signs of browning.

□ Canned pineapple, because of its metallic flavor is unworthy of any good cook's efforts. Buy the fresh product.

Kitchen Hints

□ If the fruit is just short of being ripe, you can increase the sweetness while decreasing its tartness by storing it in a pierced paper bag at room temperature for up to a few days. Pineapples that show no signs of being ripe when you buy them, however, can never be rescued: They will always be too tart for enjoyment.

□ If you are preparing pineapple rings or cubes and are inexperienced at skinning the fruit, just cut it into discs and then remove the skin.

□ Don't add raw pineapple to a gelatin mixture, because the fruit's enzymes will hinder gelling. However, if you parboil the pineapple, you deactivate the enzymes. Then, the pineapple can be incorporated into the gelatin.

□ Pineapple and cream is a splendid concoction in theory, but not in practice. Unfortunately, pineapple will cause cream to curdle.

PIZZA

☐ To give your homemade pizza a crusty bottom like the ones you eat in quality pizza parlors, line the floor of your oven with ordinary bricks or unglazed quarry tiles. Preheat the oven to 500 degrees before baking the pizza.

PLASTIC WRAP

☐ If a tight seal is critical, moisten the rim of the storage bowl before applying the plastic wrap. This technique is especially effective with glass and ceramic containers.

PLUMS

☐ Smell the plums. If you can't smell their fresh fragrance, they were picked before their time.
☐ Plums should be plump and void of bruises, cracks, soft spots, sticky surfaces, and shriveled skins.
☐ If the pit splits when you open the plums, you know the fruit has seen better days.

POACHED EGGS

☐ To keep a poaching egg from spreading too much as it cooks, spike the water with ½ teaspoon of vinegar per cup of water before you add the egg. This acidic ingredient also helps keep the albumen lily white.

POMEGRANATES

☐ A juicy pomegranate is large, heavy for its size, and has a fresh surface sheen.
☐ Reject pomegranates with cracks, blemishes, or soft spots.

☐   Pomegranates need not be refrigerated for short-term storage. Keep them in a cool, dark, well-ventilated place.

☐   Try adding pomegranate seeds to salads; they add flavor and color contrast. Incorporate them into dishes, such as chicken stews.

☐   A pomegranate should be cut in half horizontally (through its equator) rather than vertically (through its stem and blossom ends). The resulting halves will be more attractive and the seeds will be easier to remove.

POPCORN

☐   The premium popcorn brands on the market are usually worth their extra price. The resulting popcorn will be fluffier and more flavorful.

☐   Store the kernels in an airtight container and use it as soon as possible. The longer the corn is stored or exposed to air, the more it loses its moisture and the less it will expand when popped.

☐   To keep the popcorn from getting soggy, remove the lid from the pan as soon as the corn has popped.

☐   Serve and eat the popcorn while it is still very hot.

☐   The most effective way to reheat popcorn is in a covered bowl in a microwave oven.

POPPY SEEDS

☐   Reject poppy seeds which have lost their surface sheen. A dull surface indicates that the oils inside the seeds have become rancid.

☐   To help prevent rancidity, store poppy seeds in a tightly closed container in the refrigerator.

☐   For optimum flavor, poppy seeds should be toasted before adding them to preparations, such as pasta. (Pretoasting is unnecessary when you sprinkle the seeds on top of bread dough, because the baking process does the job for you.)

HOWARD HILLMAN

PORK

Marketplace Pointers

☐ The younger the pig, the more delectable and tender the flesh.

☐ You can tell the relative age of a pig by the color of its flesh. It darkens as the pig matures.

☐ Another age indicator is the bones. Those of young pigs are still slightly flexible and pink-tinted.

☐ Unless the pig was very young, its flesh should show evidence of marbling. These minute pockets of fat embedded in the lean help keep the meat succulent as it cooks.

☐ The fat layers lying next to the lean meat of young pigs are bright white without yellow pigmentation.

☐ Yet, another clue is the skin. That of a young animal will be thin and light-hued.

☐ If you see two cuts that are identical except for their size, you can be reasonably certain that the smaller specimen comes from a younger animal, and consequently, the meat will be more tender. This goes for all cuts including spare ribs.

☐ The most succulent of suckling pigs weigh less than 15 pounds.

☐ The best chop is the one whose shape resembles the beef porterhouse steak. It contains both the loin and tenderloin muscles.

☐ Select chops that are at least 1½ inches thick, or have your butcher custom cut them for you. Thin chops dry out when sautéed or broiled.

Kitchen Hints

☐ The freezer process is especially damaging to pork. Because its flesh is so lean to begin with, it will become unnecessarily dry when cooked.

☐ When you bring pork home from the store, rewrap it

loosely in butcher or wax paper. This allows the air to circulate over the meat, keeping it relatively dry.

☐ It is a common misconception that pork must be cooked to the point where all traces of pink in the flesh disappear. The meat is safe and ready to eat as soon as the color of the interior of the meat changes from a rose pink to a blush of pink. Further cooking toughens the pork.

☐ Pork tastes best when cooked to an internal temperature of 160 to 165 degrees. That level is sufficiently high to kill the trichinosis-causing parasites (which die at 137 degrees) but low enough to assure your roast doesn't dry out from overcooking.

☐ Pork chops are juicier if they are braised rather than pan-fried or broiled.

☐ Your pork roast will be easier to carve and its flesh will lose less of its juices if you let it rest for approximately 20 minutes after it comes out of the oven. This delay allows the internal juices to settle and redistribute. To keep it hot during this period, place it on a warm platter and cover it loosely with aluminum foil.

POTATO CHIPS

☐ To give a bag of potato chips a subtle new flavor, store slightly crushed, whole, peeled shallots inside the resealed bag at room temperature for 6 hours.

POTATOES

Marketplace Pointers

☐ The best potatoes for baking, mashing, and deep-frying are Idaho and other russet potatoes.

☐ The best potatoes for pan-frying, boiling, and steaming are new potatoes, whether red or white skinned.

☐ Buy new potatoes for short-term consumption. Idaho or

other russet potatoes can be kept for a week or two if properly stored.

☐ For the sake of even cooking, buy similar-sized potatoes.

☐ Leave any potato in the bin if it has green spots caused by exposure to light. These areas taste bitter and are toxic if excessive.

☐ Potato skins should be unshriveled and without sprouts or soft spots (caused by internal decay). Except for new potatoes, the skins should be 100 percent intact. Cuts and bruises should be absent or at least minimal.

☐ Sniff the potatoes for possible negative odors, such as moldiness and mustiness. There is nothing wrong with an earthy aroma, however.

☐ Potatoes purchased loose out of a bin are generally better values in the long run, because you can choose and pick, leaving the poor-conditioned specimens behind.

Kitchen Hints

☐ If you do buy prepackaged potatoes, remove any spoiled spud from the bag as soon as you get home. One bad potato can spread its affliction to the others.

☐ Never refrigerate your spuds: The low temperature will convert part of the starch content into sugar, giving the potato an unwanted flavor and texture. And, should you deep- or pan-fry the potatoes, the extra sugar will cause the spuds to darken before their interiors are thoroughly cooked.

☐ Nor is it advisable to store potatoes at room temperature (typically 68 to 75 degrees) for more than a day or two. The heat will draw out moisture, dehydrating and shriveling the spuds.

☐ Ideally, potatoes should be stored in a dark and cool (45 to 50 degrees) place that is ventilated but not drafty. Leave them exposed to the air—potatoes need to breathe.

☐   Potatoes and onions make splendid cooking but inimical storage mates. Each emits gases that negatively affect the flavor of the other.

☐   To keep potatoes from turning brown after you cut them, either start the cooking process immediately or submerge the spuds in acidulated water (1 tablespoon of vinegar or 2 tablespoons of lemon juice per quart of water).

☐   Potatoes are most nutritious if you cook and serve them unpeeled.

☐   Before cooking a potato, scrub it well with a vegetable brush. Using a paring knife or vegetable peeler, remove any sprouts or green spots on its surface and cut out any decaying areas.

☐   For cooking tips, *see* Baked Potatoes, French Fries, Hashbrowns, and Mashed Potatoes.

POTATO SALAD

☐   Potato salad should be made with new potatoes. Mature potatoes, such as the Idaho or other russets, break apart too readily and absorb too much of the vinaigrette and/or mayonnaise.

☐   Cold potato salads should be dressed as soon as you drain and cut up the potatoes. Potatoes absorb dressing more readily when they are hot.

POT HOLDERS

☐   When shopping for pot holders, your highest priority should be your hands, not your eyes. Consider issues as color coordination only after you have determined that the pot holders are well lined with a truly effective heat-retarding material, such as asbestos.

POT LIDS

☐ A blast of steam from a pot can scald you. Get in the habit of lifting the lid away from you.

☐ If you need a lid for a lidless pot, cover it with aluminum foil. To keep the rising steam from lifting the foil, set a wooden spoon or two across the top of the pot.

POTS AND PANS

☐ Invest in hanging pot racks because pots and pans stored stacked on shelves are easily dented and scratched. Pot racks also save you space and increase accessibility.

☐ Unlined cast-iron pans can darken light-hued sauces, especially if you have added wine, tomatoes, or other acidy ingredients.

☐ Don't try to lift a very hot pan with a wet cloth: Water is an excellent conductor of heat.

☐ To remove burnt food that has stuck tenaciously to the bottom of a pan, first use conventional methods to remove as much of the adhering food as you can. Then, fill the pan to the burnt level with boiling water. Mix in a generous amount of detergent or, if the food is especially burnt, powdered cleanser. Soak overnight.

Poultry. *See* Chicken, Duck, Rock Cornish Hen, and Turkey.

POUNDING MEAT

☐ Before pounding a veal cutlet or other thin, boneless slab of meat, place it inside a plastic bag. This eliminates splatter and cleanup chores.

☐ No meat pounder? Do the task with the bottom of a cast-iron skillet.

PRESERVATIVES

□ The words "no preservatives" on a package does not mean that the food is additive-free. The processor could have used chemical additives for a host of other purposes, such as coloring and flavoring.

PRICKLY PEARS

□ To assure that a prickly pear is ripe, make sure its skin hue has changed from green to yellow or red.
□ For optimum flavor, the fruit should not be too large and it should feel firm, yet slightly resilient, when squeezed.
□ Marinate cubed raw prickly pear flesh in lime juice and then add it to salads.

PRUNES

□ Some prunes sit on warm store shelves for months on end. If the prunes in your package are too chewy, they have probably lost too much moisture. Return them.
□ Once the package has been opened, the prunes must be stored in an airtight container. If you go through your prune supply slowly, refrigerate the container.
□ Don't overcook prunes, even in stews, lest they become mushy.
□ Add minced prunes to your applesauce. This gives the preparation interesting flavor, color, and texture contrasts.
□ Soak pitted prunes in a wine such as zinfadel and refrigerate overnight. Drain and serve the now plump prunes on top of vanilla ice cream for dessert.

PUDDINGS

☐   If your pudding develops a rubbery crust, scrape off this layer and cover the exposed surface of the pudding with whipped cream.

PUMPKIN

☐   A pumpkin pie requires less sugar if you use young pumpkins, those that are small for their variety. They are naturally sweeter than older ones.

☐   Younger pumpkins are also more desirable because their flesh is less fibrous.

☐   Save the pumpkin seeds. Dry them slowly in a 250-degree oven and serve them as a healthful snack.

QUICHE

☐ If your crusts are too soggy, reduce the liquid or increase the egg yolks used to make the custard mixture. Alternatively, brush the unbaked quiche shell with beaten egg 10 minutes before pouring in the custard.

QUINCES

☐ Quinces are traditionally made into jams and jellies, but they have many other culinary uses. Like apples, quinces can be cooked in pies or simply baked in the oven. Unlike apples, quinces are not eaten raw.

R

RABBIT

☐ If you plan to boil, fry, or roast a rabbit, it should not weigh more than 2½ pounds. The flesh of larger rabbits is too tough for these cooking methods.

☐ Mature rabbits are best stewed or braised.

☐ Rabbit meat is fairly lean. When roasting it, it must be barded or basted frequently.

RADISHES

☐ For the most subtly and delicately flavored red radishes, look for those with fresh green tops attached to small, bright red bulbs, which have no cracks, bruises, or soft spots.

☐ Remove the green tops, if any, to preserve the moisture in the bulbs.

☐ Keep your supply in a sealed plastic bag in the vegetable crisper.

☐ Radishes will be crisper if you soak them in ice water for an hour or two before you eat them.

RAISINS AND CURRANTS

☐ Commercially sold raisins tend to be too sweet. For a better balance of flavor and a more exciting taste, buy currants instead. Because they are smaller in size, the finished bread or other preparation will be more aesthetically pleasing.

☐ To help keep the raisins or currants plump and moist, transfer each to a tightly sealed jar as soon as you open the package. Refrigerate.

☐   Raisins and currants usually sink to the bottom of a cake or bread batter as the preparation bakes. This won't happen if you coat the dried fruit with flour before incorporating it into the batter.

☐   Plump your raisins or currants by marinating them overnight in dry sherry or Madeira.

RASPBERRIES

☐   Should the stem still be attached to the berry, the fruit was picked immaturely and, therefore, will never reach its delicious flavor potential.

☐   Reject dull-skinned raspberries. They are overripe.

☐   Never buy a box of raspberries if you see even the slightest speck of mold. That fungus spreads quickly.

☐   Sniff the container. It and the fruit should have a fresh, fruity aroma rather than a moldy or fermented one.

☐   Examine the container's bottom. If it is stained red, some of the hidden berries are crushed and may be decaying prematurely.

☐   Don't wash the raspberries until just before you use them. Surface moisture appreciably shortens their storage life.

☐   You are less likely to crush or bruise ripe raspberries when washing them if the fruit is cold rather than at room temperature.

RECIPES

☐   Index your recipes on 3- by 5-cards, giving the recipe name and its source (such as the book title and page number). File them alphabetically, by course or main ingredient.

☐   If you are attempting a recipe for the first time, a good rule of thumb is to estimate how long it will take to do the recipe, then double that time.

☐   You can save time and possible oversights if you assemble

HOWARD HILLMAN

all the ingredients for a recipe in front of you before you start cooking.

REFRIGERATION

☐ Don't put hot food into the freezer, let alone the refrigerator. The heat will foster frost build-up and raise the temperature of the other stored foods.

RHUBARB

☐ Buy rhubarb with the leaves still attached; they are freshness indicators. Look for unwilted, bright-hued leaves.
☐ The red stalks should be medium-thick and relatively firm. Reject flaccid stalks.
☐ Never cook or eat the leaves. They are poisonous.

RICE

Marketplace Pointers

☐ Instant rice is a poor substitute for regular rice. It has inferior flavor and texture—and you don't actually save any work by using it. (Regular rice takes an extra 10 minutes to cook but you don't have to tend the pot during that time.)
☐ Rather than buying preseasoned rice, purchase the regular variety and season it in your home with fresh onions and unadulterated herbs and spices. Your version will cost half as much and won't smack of chemicals.
☐ Brown rice is much more nutritious than white rice. However, if you eat a well-balanced diet, and don't rely on rice as one of your day-to-day culinary foundations, you won't suffer if you eat white rice.
☐ Converted rice lies halfway between brown and regular

white rice in terms of nutrition, but its flavor is not as praise-worthy as the other two.

Kitchen Hints

□   Rice has a shorter storage life than is commonly believed. Once you open up a package of white rice, store the grains in a tightly covered airtight container, such as a glass jar. Keep the container in a cool, dark place, and use the rice within several months.

□   Store brown rice in the refrigerator unless you plan to use it in the immediate future. Reason: Unlike white rice, brown rice still contains the nutritious germ (embryo), which becomes rancid easily at room temperature.

□   Allow extra cooking time and use more water if your rice has been stored for a long period. Rice loses moisture in storage, especially if not kept in an airtight container.

□   Brown rice takes approximately three times longer to cook than white rice, mainly because its bran covering hinders the absorption of water by the starchy interior (endosperm).

□   You need one and a half times as much water to steam brown rice as you need to steam white rice, partly because brown rice requires a longer cooking period.

□   Don't remove the lid prematurely from a pot of steaming rice, even to take a quick peek. Doing so would let the trapped steam escape. This, in turn, lowers the quality of the finished product and increases the cooking time of the rice.

□   The best test for doneness for steamed rice is to cut or bite a grain of rice in half. The rice needs further steaming if its core is still hard. You've cooked the rice too long if the grain is soft throughout.

□   When the grain you are testing has only a slight resistance, it's time to turn off the heat. Lightly fluff the rice with a fork or spoon, being careful not to crush the grains. Cover the pot and let stand for 5 minutes before serving.

☐ Leftover rice combines well with many foods. You can, for instance, make Chinese stir-fried rice or a cold rice salad. If added to soups and stews, the rice will thicken the liquid. Have you tried mixing some into the beaten eggs for an omelet?

☐ A microwave oven is particularly effective for reheating leftover rice. The rice must be covered so that the generated steam keeps the grains moist as they heat.

ROASTING

☐ Think twice about roasting meat in the same pan with vegetables such as potatoes and corn. The vegetables will yield moisture which will partially steam the meat that should be cooking with dry heat. This alters the flavor and texture of the finished roast.

ROCK CORNISH HEN

☐ The Rock Cornish hen is one of the worst values in the marketplace. On a price per pound basis, it costs significantly more than do standard-sized chickens. On a flavor basis, it is relatively bland. The bird's redeeming quality is its small size. Each diner gets his own hen.

ROLLING PIN

☐ In a country cabin without a rolling pin? Soak off the label of a tall wine or liquor bottle and fill the container with ice-cold water. Then proceed with your pastry making.

ROSEMARY

☐ Fresh rosemary is preferable to the dried variety. Of the dried types, the whole leaf is more aromatic and flavorful than the preground version.

☐ You can add dried whole rosemary leaves to slow-cooked dishes, but you should grind or chop the leaves (or put them in a removable muslin bag) for use in short-cooked preparations. Otherwise, the leaves will be too hard for the diner's comfort.

RUTABAGAS

☐ Mature rutabagas are woody and fibrous. By purchasing small specimens that are heavy for their size, you'll take home tender, delectably flavored rutabagas.

☐ Examine the skin of the rutabaga. It should be smooth and free of abrasions, discolorations, and soft spots.

☐ Unwaxed rutabagas don't have to be peeled prior to cooking and, therefore, will retain their nutrients and sweet background taste.

SAFFLOWER OIL

☐ Safflower oil is the best all around cooking oil because it has an exceptionally high smoking point, which makes the oil ideal for frying.

SAFFRON

☐ The provenience of saffron is important. The best comes from Kashmir in India. If that import is unattainable, look for Spanish saffron, which is usually commendable. Saffron from Mexico seldom is.

☐ Buy whole, not crushed saffron. Crushed saffron has lost much of its prized aromatics and, unlike whole saffron, can be adulterated easily by a shady processor.

☐ When using whole saffron, crush it in a mortar or between your fingers just before you add it to the cooking pot. Alternatively, soak the saffron in a small quantity of the cooking liquid for about 10 minutes. Press the saffron stigmata with the back of a spoon to release color and flavor, and then return the liquid and soaked saffron to the pot.

SAGE

☐ Sage can give your dishes a camphorwood flavor if it is cooked in a stew for more than an hour or two. For best results, add this herb approximately 30 minutes before the completion of the cooking period.

SALAD DRESSING

☐ Perk up and customize a commercial salad dressing by adding seasoning agents, such as fresh herbs, chopped garlic, or freshly squeezed lemon juice. A few drops of dry sherry or Madeira per serving also performs the magic.

SALADS

☐ You can reduce the amount of dressing you use in a salad if the lettuce leaves are dry. Reason: The oil in the dressing clings better to dry than wet leaves. Therefore, dry your leaves well with paper towels or, even better, with a plastic rotary-salad basket (sells for about $15 and pays for itself with the oil you save).

☐ If you mix the oil and vinegar into the salad separately, be sure you add the oil first. Should you reverse the order, most of the oil will slide off the wet leaves (vinegar is chiefly water).

☐ The ratio of oil to vinegar in a salad dressing should be at least 3 to 1. The taste would be too acidy if the ratio were lower.

☐ Your salads will be less likely to wilt on a scorching day if you chill the salad bowl.

☐ Remember, broccoli, cauliflower, and zucchini can be eaten raw—try adding some small pieces of young specimens to your next salad.

SALAMI

☐ At your next backyard party, served cubed salami accompanied by toothpicks and a mustard-based dip. Remove the salami skin (if any) and pierce the meat in several places to prevent bursting. Barbecue the sausage over low-to-moderate heat, turning frequently until it is heated through. Cube the meat and serve.

SALT

☐ Kosher salt adheres better to foods than ordinary table salt, because it has a rougher, more jagged surface. Keep some kosher salt on hand for preparations such as corn on the cob.

☐ Gourmets find the taste of sea salt (evaporated from fresh sea water) to be more enticing than ordinary table salt (mined from the dried deposits of the ancient seas).

☐ Live in a humid climate? A half dozen or so grains of uncooked white rice in a salt shaker will keep the shaker from clogging.

☐ Oversalt your dish? You can reduce the perceived degree of saltiness by adding sugar. The quantity should be small, just short of the point where you would begin to taste the sugar.

☐ You can also decrease a salty taste in a soup or stew by adding cubes or slices of uncooked potatoes. The potatoes will absorb some of the salt as they cook. If you don't want the potatoes to be part of your dish, serve them separately or save them for your next meal.

SALT PORK

☐ Salt pork is extremely salty. If you think the saltiness will throw your recipe out of kilter, blanch the salt pork before you cook with it.

☐ Alternatively, you can substitute fatback. It is less salty than salt pork.

SALT SUBSTITUTES

☐ Persons who watch their intake of salt would be better off gastronomically if they used less salt rather than switching to a commercial salt substitute. If the diet prohibits salt entirely, the individual can still eat flavorful meals by creatively substituting lemon juice, ginger, herbs and spices, and members of the onion family for the salt.

☐ Some marketing people tout potassium chloride as a salt substitute. Though it resembles salt in appearance, it doesn't taste like it, and it imparts its own curious flavor to food. Moreover, you will have created a new health problem, should your body not be able to tolerate an increased intake of potassium.

☐ If you are watching your salt intake, scrutinize the ingredients list of any processed food you buy—you could find some surprises. For example, some ground herb and spice mixtures, such as chili powder and poultry seasoning, contain salt.

SANDWICHES

☐ For an economical sandwich spread, chop your leftover meat and mix it with mayonnaise and seasonings, such as herbs, spices, and lemon juice.

☐ When making heroes (submarines or grinders or whatever they are called in your region), form a slight depression in the loaf by pulling out some of the bread's interior. This creates a convenient trough for holding a generous stack of salami, cheese, tomatoes, onions, lettuce, and the other ingredients. The stuffing is less likely to ooze out, as well.

☐ The bread of lunchbox sandwiches will be less soggy if you spread the mayonnaise and other moist condiments between the meat (or cheese) and lettuce layers, instead of directly on the bread.

SAUCES

☐ Some cooks sauté, broil, or roast meat without taking advantage of the particles that adhere to the bottom and sides of the cooking pan. These culinary treasures are the concentrated internal juices of the meat. (Think of them as free, fresh, homemade miniature bouillon cubes.) After pouring out the fat in the pan, dissolve the clinging particles over moderate heat

HOWARD HILLMAN

with a little water, stock, or wine, using a wooden spoon. Spoon the flavorful liquid over the meat before you serve it.

□ White sauces take on new dimensions in flavor and hue if you brown the flour when making the roux. Remember, though, that you need to use a little extra flour because the browning process reduces the flour's thickening power.

□ An acid ingredient, such as wine, also reduces the thickening power of a flour and other starch thickeners. Consequently, don't incorporate the acid into the sauce until near the end of the cooking period.

□ When substituting cornstarch for the white wheat flour, cut the recipe measurement in half. Cornstarch has about twice the thickening power of white wheat flour.

□ Cornstarch produces a more transparent and glistening sauce than wheat flour. On the other hand, a sauce made with white wheat flour can be cooked at a higher heat without separating.

□ A starch-thickened sauce will begin to thin if you overcook the mixture. The maximum figure is roughly 5 minutes for regular white flour and 3 minutes for cornstarch. For arrowroot, even 1 minute can be too long.

□ Don't thicken with bread flour. Because it has a high gluten content, it tends to become gummy.

□ Flour, cornstarch, and other similar thickeners will lump if added directly to hot water. Before adding the flour, convert it to a slurry (thin paste) by mixing it thoroughly in a small bowl or cup with an equal volume of cold tap water. Then, gradually warm this slurry by blending some of the hot cooking liquid into it. Finally, slowly pour the warmed slurry into the pot, stirring constantly.

□ A sauce thickened with a slurry develops a surface skin if you let the preparation stand for more than a few minutes. To prevent this from happening, stir the waiting sauce occasionally. Or place a layer of plastic wrap directly on top of the exposed surface.

□ Most lumpy sauces can be salvaged by giving them a quick

workout in your blender or food processor. Alternatively, you can press them through a sieve with a wooden spoon.

☐ Don't freeze emulsified sauces, such as hollandaise and mayonnaise; they are guaranteed to separate when thawed. So will any other sauce that has a high-fat content.

SAUSAGES

☐ It is especially important to read the ingredients list when buying sausage; so often, the product is stretched with cereal grain fillers or laden with chemicals.

☐ If you like the sound and feel of a crisp snap when you bite into a sausage, opt for those with natural as opposed to synthetic casings.

☐ Unless you plan to use a hard sausage, such as salami, within a day or two, buy it in one piece and slice it as needed. You appreciably preserve its flavor and extend its storage life.

☐ Hard sausages should be sliced as thin as your skill and knife allow.

☐ Before putting your homemade pork sausage meat into a casing, test it for seasoning. Fry a sample before tasting it, however, because of the trichinosis threat.

☐ To prevent sausages from bursting, cook them slowly and turn them frequently. Another method is to puncture the skins with the tines of a fork to allow the steam and excess fat to escape.

SAUTÉING

☐ Effective sautéing cannot be done in a saucepan. The high sides of the vessel hinder the evaporation of the water molecules released by the hot food. This means that the cooking temperature is decreased and the food partially steams.

☐ For effective browning, the meat must be at room temperature.

HOWARD HILLMAN

☐   When sautéing in butter, the best time to add the ingredients to the skillet is a few seconds after the bubbles of the sizzling butter begin to recede.

☐   Sautéing in butter poses a problem because it scorches at a much lower temperature than does cooking oil. You can raise the scorching point by adding some cooking oil to the butter.

☐   Don't crowd the food in the pan. If there is inadequate space between the individual pieces, steam is trapped underneath the food. This imprisoned moisture gives food a mushy texture and hinders the browning process.

☐   When sautéing meat, add salt at the end of the cooking process. Otherwise, this ingredient will draw out moisture from the meat. This moisture—which collects under the meat—will steam the meat and, therefore, prevent its surface from browning properly.

☐   Add spices and garlic near the end of the sautéing process. Reason: Spices and garlic tend to become bitter when fried over high heat for more than a short time.

SCALLIONS

Marketplace Pointers

☐   Some greengrocers sell immature onions as scallions. Though these members of the onion family resemble each other in appearance, the flavor of the scallion is decidedly more delicate, and, therefore, they cannot be substituted for each other in a recipe without some change in the flavor of the finished dish. Here's how to tell them apart: The base of the scallion is straight-sided, while that of the baby onion is slightly bulbous.

☐   Scallion leaves should be bright green and not flabby, clammy, split, or yellow-tinged.

☐   The white stem should be firm and unblemished and long relative to its thickness.

☐ When buying scallions in a bunch, select equal-sized specimens. The best all-purpose thickness is slightly less than ½ inch.

Kitchen Hints

☐ Remove and discard the membrane surrounding the white stem, but don't throw away the green tops. They have many culinary uses, including being chopped and added to salad dressings.

☐ Marinate trimmed scallions overnight in a seasoned vinegar and oil dressing. Serve as an appetizer.

☐ Scallions are usually eaten raw, but they are also a treat when braised in butter and served as a vegetable side dish.

☐ Don't sauté chopped scallions for more than a minute or they may scorch.

SCALLOPS

Marketplace Pointers

☐ The scallops should smell ocean fresh. They should be plump and, when pressed, resilient.

☐ The small bay scallop (about ½ inch in diameter) costs more than the larger ocean (sea) scallop (approximately 1½ inches in diameter) but is more succulent, sweeter, and less chewy.

☐ A few merchants have been known to fool their customers by stamping bay scallop-sized discs out of firm fish fillets. Alternatively, they cut up ocean scallops into pieces the size of bay scallops.

☐ Some greedy merchants increase the weight of their scallops by soaking them before they sell them. This ruse is easily detected: The scallops are exceptionally white and usually sit in a shallow pool of their secreted water.

HOWARD HILLMAN

Kitchen Hints

☐ Cooked scallops are often tough because the cook didn't seal in the internal juices by first searing the flesh quickly in hot oil or butter.

☐ Another cause of toughness is overcooking. Once seared, reduce the heat to a moderate setting. Then cook bay scallops for only 2 to 3 minutes, depending on their thickness.

SCRAMBLED EGGS AND OMELETS

☐ Scrambled eggs and omelets will have better textures if you don't overbeat them.

☐ Scrambled eggs or omelets will be fluffier if you add a teaspoon of water, milk, or cream per egg before you start to beat the mixture. Reason: The liquid steams, creating tiny air pockets in the eggs. For a special flavor, add 1 teaspoon of dry vermouth per egg, instead.

☐ Unlike omelets, scrambled eggs should never be cooked over high heat. Notice, for instance, how much less rubbery the whites of your fried eggs are when you cook them slowly over low-to-moderate heat.

SESAME OIL

☐ Sesame oil lends an enticing flavor to salads and sautéed foods if it is used in small quantities. Use it with other oils on a 1-to-5 basis. Because its aromatics are quite volatile, add it near the end of the cooking process.

SESAME SEEDS

☐ Sprinkle roasted or toasted white sesame seeds over cooked green vegetables, such as spinach, for color contrast, added flavor, and texture.

☐ Store your supply of sesame seeds in an airtight container in the refrigerator. Because the seeds contain oil, they can become rancid quickly at room temperature.

SHALLOTS

☐ There is no substitute for fresh shallots. The dehydrated minced or powdered products won't do justice to your dishes.
☐ The skins should be unblemished, snugly encasing the firm, plump flesh.
☐ You are not using up your shallot supply quickly enough if they begin to sprout.
☐ The term "1 shallot" in a recipe traditionally means 1 medium-sized clove, not the whole bulb.
☐ The smaller variety of shallots tend to have the most intense flavor. On an ounce-per-ounce basis, however, the larger ones require less peeling time.
☐ Shallots should never be sautéed for more than a minute or two because they scorch easily.

Sherbet. *See* Ice Cream.

SHERRY

☐ Sherry should be added to a soup immediately before you serve the preparation. Otherwise, much of the fortified wine's delicate fragrance will dissipate into the air before you take your first sip.
☐ The amount of sherry you add to a soup should be modest—no more than 1 teaspoon per cup. Otherwise, you will be tasting the sherry more than the soup.

SHOPPING LIST

☐ Buy a brightly colored set of 3- by 5-inch cards expressly for the kitchen. Use them to form lists of the items you need.

Keep the current card handy in one specific location (a certain drawer, on your bulletin board, wherever) and reserve the color strictly for this use. It works.

SHRIMP

Marketplace Pointers

☐   Smell the shrimp. They should smell ocean fresh, not fishy or of ammonia. Don't buy shrimp that have more than a slight iodine odor as that could suggest that iodine has been used as a preservative.

☐   Fresh shrimp are far superior to frozen shrimp. When cooked, frozen shrimp will have a mushy texture and bland flavor.

☐   Should you have to buy frozen shrimp, examine the individual shrimps in the plastic pouch closely. If they are shelled, each shrimp should be encased in its own relatively thick ice layer. If they are unshelled, the flesh should fit snugly in the carapace (the longer a shrimp is stored, the more its flesh shrinks).

☐   Jumbo shrimp varieties cost more than their smaller cousins. However, unless you plan to stuff the large-sized shrimp, consider buying the same weight of a smaller shrimp. Though the latter do demand more preparation time, because of deveining, they usually are more tender and subtly flavored.

Kitchen Hints

☐   It is not necessary to devein a shrimp for your health's sake. However, the shrimp will be more aesthetically pleasing on the table if you do. (Remember the intestinal vein is not the black nerve cord that runs down the inside curve of the shrimp, but rather the one that runs down the exterior curve.)

☐ It's best to cook a shrimp in its shell. The carapace adds subtle flavor to the flesh.

☐ Simmer, never boil, shrimp, as boiling toughens the flesh. So does overcooking.

☐ Unshelled shrimp need to simmer for only 3 to 6 minutes and shelled ones, 2 to 5 minutes, depending on their size. Shrimp are cooked when the shells or the shelled flesh start to turn pink.

☐ Virtually all of the crustaceans sold in this country as "prawns" or "scampi" are really jumbo shrimp. The true prawn has a pair of lobster-like claws and a well deserved gastronomic reputation.

SICHUAN (SZECHWAN) PEPPERCORNS

☐ Use a regular peppermill for storing and grinding whole buds of this Chinese spice.

SIEVES

☐ Inexpensive metal sieves usually dent and discolor within the year. Buy quality.

☐ The conical sieve is better than the bowl-shaped one for straining stocks and soups. Reason: It's easier to press out the flavorful juices of the food solids in the liquid if those solids are concentrated in one central location. For best results, use the conical-tipped pestle that normally comes with the sieve.

☐ Always wash sieves promptly after using them. Once food particles dry within the mesh, it's difficult to dislodge them, even with prolonged soaking and scrubbing.

SNAILS

☐ Snails raised in France have better flavor than those gathered in the Balkans and the Far East. If you see the word *azatine* on the container, the contents are not the prized French escargot.

☐ Here's how to recycle the shells. Boil them for 60 minutes in salted water containing baking soda. Drain and air dry.

☐ Shells aren't necessary. Coat the snails with a butter-based seasoned sauce and bake them in mushroom caps basted with butter in a preheated 300-degree oven for approximately 10 minutes.

SNOWPEAS

☐ Snowpeas, at their best, are crisp, vivid green, unblemished, and relatively small.

☐ Frozen snowpeas are too flaccid to be considered a suitable substitute for the fresh ones.

☐ When preparing snowpeas, be sure to remove the natural thread that runs along one of the edges. It's edible but too fibrous.

SOFT-SHELL CRABS

☐ The soft-shell crab season runs from late spring through summer.

☐ The best time to plan a soft-shell crab dinner is shortly after a full moon. The supply is generally larger (and, therefore, less expensive) during that part of the lunar month, because crabs tend to molt most during a full moon.

SORREL

☐ Though sorrel usually ends up as the star ingredient in a cream soup, its leaves can be eaten raw in salads if they are young and tender.

SOUR CREAM

☐ If you cook a mixture containing sour cream at a temperature higher than a simmer, the sour cream will probably curdle and separate.

SPINACH

Marketplace Pointers

☐ Always sniff prepackaged spinach for telltale signs of deterioration. Too often the contents have turned sour before the customer takes it out of the store.

☐ Loose spinach is almost always better than prepackaged fresh spinach. But, again, you must use the sniff test.

☐ Spinach leaves should be a deep, vivid green and free of wilting and insect damage. The leaves should be slightly moist but not slimy.

☐ The smaller the spinach plant or leaves, the more tender and delicately flavored the vegetable will be. Look for short, stout leaf bunches.

☐ Fresh spinach is at its best during the cool winter months. Perfect summertime spinach is difficult to find.

☐ Spinach is one of the few vegetables that freezes and thaws reasonably well. It's no gastronomic sin to use frozen spinach when prime-condition fresh spinach is unavailable.

☐ Fresh spinach is more perishable than commonly believed. Store it, unwashed, in a sealed plastic bag in the vegetable crisper and use it within a day or two.

Kitchen Hints

☐ The natural bitter flavor of spinach is amplified by overcooking. Cook spinach only to the point that it begins to shrink and its color intensifies.

☐ For the sake of preserving the nutrients, don't add any water to the pot. The moisture that clings to the spinach leaves after you wash them provides ample liquid.

☐ If you are going to serve the steamed spinach with other foods on the same plate, lightly squeeze the cooked spinach before you serve it. You will rid the spinach of excess moisture that would otherwise flow into the other food on the plate, adulterating their flavors.

☐ The best way to serve steamed spinach is in small individual serving bowls. In this way, you don't need to squeeze the spinach before you serve it.

☐ Contrary to widespread belief, eating spinach raw is less nutritious than eating it cooked. Reason: The cellular walls of spinach are rather hard compared to those of most of the other vegetables that can be eaten raw. Consequently, many of the vitamins and nutrients of the spinach pass through your digestive system imprisoned within these cells. By cooking spinach, you break down these cellular walls, allowing more of the nutrients to escape and be absorbed by your digestive system.

Spring Onions. *See* Scallions.

SQUAB

☐ Buy one squab per diner.

☐ The most tender fleshed squab weighs 1 pound or less. Heavier ones are well on their way to becoming mature pigeons, undesirable tablefare.

☐ Squab, being relatively small, should be roasted in a preheated 400-degree oven. Baste them frequently. Cook for 30 to 40 minutes.

☐ Here's another clue for spotting an older bird: Its flesh will be darker-hued and its breastbone less pliable.

SQUASH BLOSSOMS

☐ The flowers of zucchini and other popular squashes are delicious. You can add them raw to salads, sauté them in olive oil, or dip them in batter and deep-fry them.

SQUID

☐ To make sure you are purchasing a fresh squid, as opposed to one that has been frozen and thawed, examine its eyes— they should look bright and alert. Also scrutinize the body: The flesh should be semi-firm and slime-free, and the purple dappled outer membrane should be reasonably intact.

☐ Choose the smallest specimens for their species; the meat is more tender.

☐ Young squid are already tender enough to eat raw. (Sushi lovers order them.) One cooks a young squid only to augment its flavor. Sauté or fry the flesh for no more than a minute or two. Longer cooking toughens the tender meat.

☐ Mature squid should not be sautéed or fried. Gently simmer (don't boil) them for 20 minutes to 2 hours, depending on the thickness of the pieces.

☐ For a cool summer salad, slice the squid into rings. Sauté briefly or deep-fry the pieces and marinate them overnight in a vinaigrette sauce. Garnish with minced sweet red peppers and chopped fresh parsley or basil leaves.

Star Anise. *See* Anise Seeds.

STEAMING

☐ The most nutritious method for cooking vegetables is steaming.

HOWARD HILLMAN

☐ One of the least expensive yet most useful pieces of equipment is the small metal vegetable steaming basket. If possible, buy one with a removable stem handle. It not only allows you to steam large pieces, but it accommodates more food.

☐ The number one secret of steaming is not to oversteam. When cooking broccoli, for instance, turn off the heat and uncover the pot the moment this vegetable becomes a vivid green. By doing so, you preserve flavor, nutrients, color, and texture.

STEWS

☐ If you have not browned the meat for a stew, always bring the liquid to a simmer before you add the meat. The heat helps seal in the precious meat juices and flavor.

☐ To thicken a stew quickly, add a small quantity of pastina (grain-sized soup pasta) approximately 10 minutes before the dish is finished.

☐ Calorie- and cholesterol-watchers can eliminate most of the fat in a stew by cooking the dish the day before. The fat will collect in a firm, easily removable layer on top of the stew during its overnight stay in the refrigerator.

☐ Cook twice as much meat stew as you plan to eat for the meal. Leftover meat stew is desirable because its flavor improves with time.

☐ If the fish pieces in your fish stew break apart into small morsels, serve the stew over a bed of rice.

STOCK

☐ Bouillon cubes are a poor substitute for homemade stocks made with fresh bones. The commercial products smack of the chemicals they contain.

☐ Bones should be cracked (by the butcher or you) before you use them for making soup or stock. This facilitates the release of their flavor and collagen, a thickening agent.

☐ Unless from a very young animal, pork and lamb bones will give a stock a very pronounced flavor that is not to everyone's taste.

☐ Veal bones make a clearer and more delicate stock than do beef bones. Veal bones also have a higher gelatin content, an important consideration when making aspics.

☐ For delicate-flavored chicken stocks, choose breast over leg or neck bones and young over mature birds. For full-flavored stocks, do the opposite.

☐ The closer the anatomical position of a bone to the nose, tail, or foot, the more thickening power it has.

☐ Your beef stock will have a deeper flavor and hue if you roast the bones in a 400-degree oven for 20 minutes before using them.

☐ Bones of roasted beef, pork, lamb, veal, or poultry are not ideal for making stock. Much of their flavor has been absorbed by the cooking meat.

☐ If you want to remove virtually all the fat from a homemade stock, refrigerate the preparation overnight. By the next day, the fat will have coagulated into an easy-to-remove layer on top of the stock.

☐ A quicker but less efficient method of degreasing a stock is to use a baster, the utensil that resembles an oversized eyedropper. Or you could use paper towels to soak up some of the floating fat. Note: The so-called skimming spoons and ladles with the oversized holes are not effective.

STRAWBERRIES

☐ Look for strawberries that are more spherical than conical.

☐ Fresh strawberries should be vivid and red without any remaining traces of green or yellow.

☐ The best strawberries will still be sporting their green caps and be free of mold or bruises.

☐ The scent of fresh strawberries should be pleasingly fragrant, not absent or sour.

☐ Finally, good strawberries are small for their variety as larger ones tend to have balsawood textures.

☐ Because strawberries develop mold quickly, they should be purchased for short-term consumption and stored unwashed.

☐ Wash strawberries unhulled and do it quickly but gently. Soaking makes them waterlogged.

String Beans. *See* Green Beans.

STUFFINGS

☐ Bread stuffing will ooze out of a bird if you stuff the cavity to more than 80 percent of its capacity. Reason: Bread stuffing expands as it cooks.

☐ When stuffing a fatty bird, such as a duck or goose, don't plan to eat the stuffing. The stuffing mixture absorbs too much of the fat.

☐ If you refrigerate or freeze a cooked bird without first removing its stuffing, that encasing may become bacterially contaminated before it has a chance to cool. Always store the stuffing separately and do it promptly after the meal.

SUGAR

☐ The best all-around sugar for the kitchen is the superfine (extra-fine) variety. It dissolves more quickly than granulated sugar.

☐ Should your recipe call for superfine sugar and you have

only the granulated variety in your cupboard, give it a whirl in your food processor or blender.

☐ Don't use powdered sugar to sweeten drinks. It has a tendency to lump. Powdered sugar will also fog your drinks if cornstarch has been combined with it by the processor to prevent caking. (Read the label.)

☐ *See also* Brown Sugar, Icing, Sugar Substitutes.

SUGAR SUBSTITUTES

☐ Sugar substitute products have an ungratifying flavor. Unless your doctor prohibits sugar in your diet, it is better to cut back on the quantity of sugar you use than to debase the taste of your preparation with a sugar substitute. Save your calories elsewhere.

SUSHI AND SASHIMI

☐ Under no circumstances should you eat raw freshwater fish. It's too risky, even for a daredevil gourmet.

☐ Raw ocean fish can be safe to eat if the fish was caught within the past 24 hours in non-polluted waters and handled with utmost hygienic care. However, since virtually all the fish sold in American fish markets fall short of that standard, you must proceed with caution. Hepatitis is one of the looming dangers.

SWEETBREADS

Marketplace Pointers

☐ The sweetbreads from younger animals are more tender and delicate than those from older ones. The hue of this variety of meat provides a clue to age: As the animal grows older, its sweetbreads lose their whiteness and acquire a red tint.

☐ Select plump sweetbreads. They should be free of off odors.

☐ Buy only for immediate consumption, as sweetbreads are quite perishable.

Kitchen Hints

☐ The traces of blood in sweetbreads will turn brown when cooked. To help eliminate this cosmetic problem, soak the sweetbreads in acidulated water (1 tablespoon of vinegar or 2 of lemon juice per quart of cool water) for an hour or two before cooking.

☐ To help sweetbreads maintain their shape and keep them whole while they are being sautéed or broiled, first blanch them in simmering water.

☐ If you do soak and/or blanch the sweetbreads, rid them of their excess moisture before you sauté or broil them. To accomplish this, weight them down with a heavy plate for a couple of hours in the refrigerator.

SWEET PEPPERS

☐ Because the interior of a sweet pepper rots rapidly, it's important to know how to identify the freshest specimen. The exterior should be firm, unshriveled, bright-hued, and free of any cuts or discoloration. The pepper should be heavy for its size.

☐ Select well-proportioned sweet peppers; they will be easier to prepare whether you are cutting or stuffing them.

☐ The Italian sweet pepper is gastronomically superior to the common bell pepper. The first can be easily recognized by its elongated shape; the latter is bulbous.

☐ Sweet peppers are best stored sealed in a plastic bag in the vegetable crisper.

☐ Besides removing the seeds, always cut out and discard the bitter membranes.

☐ To skin a whole sweet red or green pepper, first evenly char the skin in your broiler. Then pop the vegetable into a brown paper bag. Close the bag tightly and let stand for 5 minutes as the developing steam helps loosen the scorched skin. Finally, peel off the skin under cool running water.

☐ Before stuffing and baking a sweet pepper, soften it by parboiling it for 5 minutes.

☐ Baked stuffed sweet peppers will dry out unless they are first rubbed with oil, or are cooked surrounded by a liquid.

☐ Overcooked sweet peppers lose their appealing vivid hue and may become bitter.

SWEET POTATOES

☐ Not all sweet potatoes on the market taste alike. The most popular variety, sometimes called a "yam," has a brownish-orange skin and coral-orange flesh. It is sweeter and has a moister, less mealy texture than the one with the paler skin and flesh.

☐ For baking whole, the variety with the paler skin and flesh should be your choice. For boiling and mashing, the coral-orange fleshed sweet potato is preferable.

☐ Mature sweet potatoes are too fibrous for good eating. Buy specimens that are medium-sized or smaller for their variety.

☐ Select sweet potatoes with skins free of abrasions and soft spots—as deterioration can permeate their flesh quickly.

☐ Never refrigerate a sweet potato as cold temperatures convert some of the vegetable's starch into sugar. This changes not only the flavor but the cooking properties of the sweet potato as well.

HOWARD HILLMAN

☐   The proper storage environment for a sweet potato is a cool (about 55 degrees), dry, well-ventilated place.

☐   To preserve flavor and nutrients, cook sweet potatoes in their jackets.

T

TABLE MANNERS

☐ If you are standing when serving food to a diner, position yourself to his left. However, you should stand on his right side when pouring a beverage, because glasses are traditionally placed on the right.

☐ Foods and beverages should be passed clockwise around the table.

TAKE-OUT FOODS

☐ The carryout "gourmet food" sections in stores can be a convenience for working people. But before you pay your cash, look for negative signs, such as soggy salads, brownish crusts forming on the food in the display pans, and the overall hygiene of the employees and facilities.

TASTING

☐ When testing a food for seasoning, pay particular attention to your first smell or taste. Your second sampling, if it closely follows the first, will not reveal as much information, because your senses will have become partially desensitized.

TEA

Marketplace Pointers

☐ Whole loose tea has a maximum storage life of 1 year if stored in an airtight container in a cool, dark place. Tea bags have markedly shorter storage lives—buy for only short-term consumption.

☐ If you can crumble the tea into powder with your fingers, it has lost its freshness.

☐ Tea bags are convenient, but loose tea makes the best brew.

☐ In descending order of quality, loose tea is classified as whole (leaf), broken, or powdered. The whole leaves are best, because they retain more of their aromatic oils.

☐ Whole tea leaves should be uniform in size and small for their variety.

Kitchen Hints

☐ Always preheat the tea pot before brewing the tea.

☐ Tea should be made with simmering, not boiling, water because a 212-degree temperature brings out the bitterness in the leaves.

☐ Prolonged steeping also produces a bitter, harsh tea. For most loose teas, a 5-minute brewing period yields the best results.

☐ Don't stir the tea during the steeping period. Should you need to stir the leaves after the tea is brewed, do it gently.

☐ If you want a stronger cup of tea, increase the quantity of tea, not the brewing period.

☐ The average cup of tea has half the caffein of an equivalent volume of coffee.

☐ See also Iced Tea.

THAWING MEAT

☐ Meat should be thawed in the refrigerator, not at room temperature.

☐ If you will be away for the day and need to defrost a 5-pound piece of meat for the evening's meal, select a cooler that has a volume of approximately twice that of the meat. Insert the meat, cover the cooler, and let it sit on the kitchen counter. By the time you come home, the meat should be thawed—or nearly so—and still be wholesome.

☐ If you plan to marinate a thawed piece of meat, why not let it marinate as it thaws. Place both the frozen meat and the marinade in a plastic bag in the refrigerator. Turn the bag occasionally.

THYME

☐ Thyme is one of the few herbs that is excellent in both the garden fresh and the crushed dried forms. Powdered dried thyme is undesirable, because it quickly loses its aromatics.

☐ Thyme is called the "workhorse" herb for good reason. It harmonizes with many cooking ingredients and is compatible with most other seasoning agents, including bay leaf.

Tofu. *See* Bean Curd.

TOMATOES

Marketplace Pointers

☐ The best tomato for cooking is the vine-ripened variety. If this tomato is unavailable, substitute a quality brand of canned plum tomatoes. The cottony, gas-ripened tomatoes that are sold in supermarkets fall too short in texture and flavor to even consider cooking with them. Eating them raw is also unexciting, gastronomically speaking.

☐ Always sniff a tomato before you buy it. Reject it if it lacks a fragrant scent.

☐ If the tomatoes are slightly underripe, store them in a pierced paper bag at room temperature for a day or two. Once ripened, use immediately or refrigerate or store in a cool cellar.

HOWARD HILLMAN

Kitchen Hints

☐ Store-bought tomatoes must be washed gently but thoroughly with a vegetable brush or nylon scouring pad to help rid them of any possible chemical coating. Giving them only a quick rinse before adding them to a salad or cooking pot is taking an unnecessary risk.

☐ When cooking whole or quartered tomatoes in a sauce, soup, or stew, you must either peel them ahead of time or strain the preparation afterwards. Otherwise, the diner will be eating the shriveled, unchewable stringy skins.

☐ To peel tomatoes, place them in a pot of boiling water and let them stand for 15 to 60 seconds, depending on their size. Immediately remove the tomatoes and submerge them in a bowl of cold water. The skins will come off easily if the tomatoes are reasonably ripe and mature.

☐ Generally, you don't have to peel tomatoes for cooking purposes if you first chop them. Reason: The skin pieces are so small to begin with that they will shrivel into bits.

☐ When preparing a tomato for a salad, cut it into wedges rather than slices if you want to minimize the amount of juice that coats the leaves and dilutes the salad dressing.

☐ Don't cook tomatoes in untreated aluminum or cast-iron pots. The acid in the tomato chemically reacts with the aluminum or iron, giving the tomatoes a brownish tinge. Even the flavor of the dish is affected.

TOMATO JUICE

☐ For a change of pace, give your tomato (or orange) juice a spin in the blender. The generated frothiness adds new visual and textural dimensions.

TOMATO PASTE

☐ Commercial tubes of tomato paste are handy and economical when you need only a small amount for a dish.

☐ If you want to save even more money, transfer some of your leftover tomato paste into a camper's reusable squeeze tube (available at many sporting good stores). Keep refrigerated.

TONGUE

☐ For the most tender meat, select a tongue that is relatively small. Cook it with slow, moist heat (braising or simmering) and slice it thinly across the grain.

☐ It will be easier to slice thin pieces if you let the tongue cool, and begin at the tip end.

TORTILLAS

☐ Warming store-bought tortillas is tricky because they dry out easily when heated. For a crispy exterior (but still moist interior), heat the tortillas on top of a moderately hot griddle or over a low burner flame, turning them every few seconds.

☐ For a soft-texture, heat the tortillas with steam rather than direct heat. Stack the tortillas in a vegetable steamer and place this metal basket in a pot containing ½ inch of boiling water. Cover and remove when the tortillas are heated through.

☐ You can also heat tortillas in a colander lined with a dish towel—over a pot of simmering water. Fold the excess towel in over the tortillas and top the colander with a lid. This works especially well with flour tortillas.

TRIPE

☐ Unless the tripe is relatively white, thick, and honey-combed, it may not turn out as tender and delicately flavored as you may have hoped.

☐ Even perfect tripe will toughen if you boil rather than simmer or braise it.

TRUFFLES

☐ Fresh truffles begin to lose their tantalizing aroma the minute they are unearthed. If prolonged storage is necessary, cover them in a glass jar with a neutral spirit, such as a mild-scented vodka; then refrigerate them up to a couple of weeks. Under no circumstance should you freeze them for that would annihilate the flavor subtleties you paid so dearly for.

TRUSSING NEEDLES

☐ Protect the points of these needles by storing them embedded in a wine cork.
☐ A curved carpet needle is perfect for trussing poultry.

TUNA

☐ Tuna packed in water not only has fewer calories than tuna packed in oil, it also does not have the taste of inferior oil. (Most producers pack their tuna in a relatively low-grade vegetable oil.)
☐ Making tunafish sandwiches? Save money by buying the "flake" rather than the more expensive "chunk" or "solid" tuna. After all, you are going to end up flaking the larger-sized pieces of the "chunk" and "solid" tuna with your mixing fork.
☐ For tuna salads served on lettuce leaves, you probably will want to pay the premium for the "solid" (or "fancy") or at least for the "chunk" tuna. If you want the whitest meat, choose "white meat tuna" (from the albacore species) rather than "light meat tuna."

TURKEY

Marketplace Pointers

☐ For holiday meals, you'll need roughly 1½ to 2 pounds of whole turkey per diner. For eight persons, shop for a 12 to 16 pound turkey.

☐ The larger the turkey, the more edible meat and less bone waste it will have per pound of weight. On the other hand, the younger the turkey, the more tender and delicate its flavor.

☐ Self-basting turkeys are not ideal choices. When cooked, the flesh smacks of the chemicals and other ingredients that were injected into the bird during processing. When the meat cooks, that mixture coagulates, making leftovers, such as cold turkey, uninviting. To add injury to insult, self-basting turkeys have a premium price.

☐ Avoid frozen turkeys, if possible, because when cooked, they won't be as tender and flavorful as fresh ones.

☐ If you must buy a frozen turkey, be sure to allow sufficient time to thaw it in the refrigerator. Room-temperature thawing poses a health risk. Plan on one day for a 6 pounder to three days for a 22 pounder.

Kitchen Hints

☐ Remove the turkey from the refrigerator approximately 1 hour before you put it in the oven.

☐ Allow 20 minutes plus approximately 15 minutes per pound in a preheated 325-degree oven. Subtract 2 or 3 minutes per pound for an unstuffed turkey.

☐ Despite what some cookbooks recommend, do not place aluminum foil over the turkey breast as it cooks. The foil traps steam and, consequently, the breast will acquire a mushy texture. Your best bet is to cover the breast with a butter-soaked double layer of cheesecloth and to baste it often. For a crisp brown skin, remove this cheesecloth 30 to 45 minutes before the turkey is done.

☐   Always let a roast turkey rest for 20 to 30 minutes (depending on its size) before you carve it. Place it on a warm platter and loosely cover the bird with aluminum foil. The breast will be juicier, more tender, and easier to carve because you have allowed the internal juices to settle.

TURNIPS

☐   Given a choice, buy turnips with their tops still attached, providing that the greens are unwilted and vividly hued.

☐   Have the greengrocer twist off the tops to keep the leaves from draining the juices out of the turnips. (If the leaves are fresh and from a young plant, take them home with you. They are delicious when simmered, steamed, or sautéed.)

☐   Mature (large) turnips have been partially responsible for giving this vegetable its undeserved bad reputation. Overcooking is equally to blame.

☐   For turnips at their delicate best, buy small specimens with unmarred skins. Stew or simmer them for only 15 to 25 minutes, depending on their thickness—they should retain some texture.

☐   Cooked in their skins, turnips will better retain their nutritional value and natural sweet taste.

TWEEZERS

☐   Keep a pair of tweezers in the kitchen for removing small pieces of trussing string from stuffed poultry and fish. This implement is also useful for removing tiny bones from fish fillets and steaks.

V

VANILLA EXTRACT

☐ There's no comparison between the aroma and flavor of real and pseudo "vanilla extract." If you see the phrase "vanilla flavoring" or "artificial vanilla" on the label, you know the product is not the genuine article.

VEAL

Marketplace Pointers

☐ There are three main types of bovine meat in the marketplace: veal (the meat from a calf under 3 months old); baby beef (3 to 12 months); and beef (1 year or older). Both veal and beef are excellent in their own separate ways: Veal is delicate and tender and beef is hearty and flavorful. Baby beef, though, has no extraordinary qualities to excite a serious palate.

☐ Unfortunately, a fair share of the "veal" sold is really baby beef. One way to spot this ruse is to note the color of the flesh. If it's creamy pink, it's veal; if it's creamy red, it's baby beef. The deepening of the red tone occurs because of the calf's increased consumption of iron in its diet.

☐ The surrounding fat (if any) is another age indicator. The whiter and less yellow it is, the younger the animal.

☐ The texture of the flesh should be relatively firm yet velvety. As the meat sits around in the meat case, the flesh loses its fresh glow and develops a brownish tint.

☐ The most tender (and expensive) veal cutlets come from the top part of the leg. If your butcher sells cutlets from the shoulder, make sure his price reflects the lesser quality.

198

□   For the sake of tenderness, the cutlet (scaloppini) should be cut across, rather than with, the grain.

□   Buy veal only for short-term consumption. Veal is more perishable than beef.

Kitchen Hints

□   Even tender leg cutlets benefit from pounding before cooking. Two secrets of successful pounding are to use a steady moderate stroke and to start at the center of the cut, moving outward.

□   Braising is the best cooking method for a veal chop. For optimum succulence, the chops should be thick.

□   Unlike beef, veal should not be cooked to a rare or medium-rare stage of doneness. It needs ample cooking to develop its delicate flavor. Overcooking, though, can drastically toughen the meat.

□   A roast is best cooked to an internal temperature of 160 degrees, when the juices begin to run clear.

□   Veal cutlets taste better if they are breaded or simply floured. These coverings enhance flavor and help seal in the juices. Breading also adds texture.

□   Veal profits even more than beef from a sauce made from the pan juices.

□   Because ground veal is lean, it can dry out when cooked unless you enrich it with a fat. The Scandinavians blend it with the fattier ground meats of pork and beef.

VEGETABLES

□   Green vegetables, such as peas and green beans, are generally best cooked with a minimum of vinegar, lemon juice, or other acidic ingredients. Reason: The acid can change the vivid green hue of these chlorophyll-rich vegetables, into an unappetizing olive-drab color.

☐ White vegetables, such as cauliflower, generally benefit when cooked with acidic ingredients. Acid helps keep these vegetables from turning yellow. If your water supply has a high alkaline content, the use of acids as an anti-yellowing measure is particularly recommended.

☐ Orange and yellow-orange vegetables, such as carrots, gain their color from carotene, which the body converts into vitamin A. If these vegetables are overcooked, the heat denatures the carotene and, therefore, the nutritional benefit is lost.

☐ With few exceptions, vegetables should be blanched before freezing them. This parboiling deactivates the enzymes, prolonging storage life and preserving color, flavor, texture, and nutrients.

☐ Green vegetables (especially green beans) can be given a vivid green hue by adding baking soda to the cooking water. However, this ploy—often used in restaurants—should be avoided because it gives vegetables a flabby texture and destroys their vitamin A content.

W

WALNUT OIL

☐ Walnut oil is the most elegant of oils to use for making salad dressings, because of its delicate walnut flavor and aroma. This accolade applies only to the quality brands, because mundane ones are so overprocessed, they are rather bland.

☐ Walnut oil turns rancid quickly, and, therefore, must be refrigerated once it is opened.

WATER

☐ Never use hot tap water for cooking or making beverages. Chances are, it has picked up an off flavor from the hot water boiler and pipes.

☐ If you have not drawn water from your cold tap within the past few hours, let it run for a short period if you plan to cook with it. Otherwise, your dish or beverage may pick up the taste of the water pipes.

☐ If you chill your tap water in the refrigerator, store it in a glass, instead of a plastic container. Plastic can give water an off flavor.

☐ Your tea or coffee will be less appealing if you make it with water that has been reboiled. Reason: Reboiled water has lost oxygen, which gives tea or coffee a lively taste.

☐ Foods are more tender if they are cooked in soft rather than hard water. If your water supply has a relatively high mineral content, consider using bottled spring water for cooking important dishes.

☐ Water will come to a boil faster, thereby saving fuel energy, if you cover the pot. The lid traps the rising steam.

☐ The higher the altitude, the longer you must boil foods.

For every 1,000 feet above sea level, the boiling point of water decreases by approximately 2 degrees. This means that boiling water in Albuquerque (4,958 feet) will be about 10 degrees cooler than boiling water in Miami (sea level).

☐ Should there be a time when you doubt the wholesomeness of your water supply, boil each batch for at least 20 minutes.

WATERCRESS

☐ Smell the greens. There should be no hint of sourness. The leaves should be vivid green with a moderate sheen.

☐ Store watercress stem side down in ½ inch of water in a sealed jar in the refrigerator.

☐ Watercress is typically purchased as a salad green, but it's also excellent when briefly sautéed in butter or used as the star ingredient in a soup.

WATERMELON

☐ Because watermelon doesn't mature once it's picked, it's important to learn ripeness and maturity indicators.

☐ If a whole watermelon is mature and ripe, it should have a creamy white underbelly, be heavy for its size, and emit a deep resonant hollow sound when slapped with your palm.

☐ Press the two ends of a whole watermelon. They should yield slightly.

☐ The surface of a whole watermelon should be dull, not glossy. Your fingernails should leave visible trails when you scrape them across the rind.

☐ When buying cut watermelon, examine the seeds. A mature watermelon has hard, black seeds. An immature one has a number of soft, white seeds.

☐ The flesh should be a bright, deep, rosy red. White streaks in the flesh indicate immaturity.

HOWARD HILLMAN

☐ A mushy, fibrous, grainy, or dry texture means the watermelon is past its prime. Look for firm, juicy flesh.

☐ Watermelon cubes make a colorful addition to fruit salads, but, unfortunately, they make the mixture too watery unless it is served promptly.

☐ *See also* Melons.

WAXED FRUITS AND VEGETABLES

☐ Think twice about buying apples, cucumbers, eggplants, peppers, potatoes, squash, sweet potatoes, tomatoes, turnips, and similar fruits and vegetables if they have been waxed.

☐ For the above reason, complain if you see your greengrocer selling waxed fruits and vegetables. If enough consumers do, then the trend toward waxing anything that resides in a produce bin will reverse itself. Though food scientists assure us that the wax is edible, this coating can trap a layer of insecticides between it and the peel. Unfortunately, you can't completely wash off the insecticides because you can't scrub off all the wax unless you use hot detergent water. Since this measure would affect negatively the flavor of the produce, you are forced to peel the fruit or vegetable for your health's sake. In the process, the nutrients that lie just under the skin are lost.

WAX PAPER

☐ Out of wax paper and your recipe requires it? Use the wax paper liner in a cereal box (transfer its contents to a glass jar).

Whipped Potatoes. *See* Mashed Potatoes.

WINE

☐ You'll do more damage than good to your food if you season it with one of those cooking wines merchandised in supermarkets. They are loaded with offensive flavoring agents. Instead, use a true wine.

☐ You need not necessarily cook with an expensive wine. Just be sure it's good enough to be enjoyed out of the glass.

☐ The wine you cook with and the wine you drink at the table can be different wines as long as they share qualities that make them compatible.

☐ Mothers of young children need not refrain from cooking with wine. The alcohol evaporates during the cooking process.

☐ Even in dishes such as coq au vin, the flavor of a wine should never dominate the dish.

☐ Wines should be added to stews at least 30 minutes before the dish is finished cooking. This permits the wine and the other ingredients to interact, creating new flavor dimensions.

☐ The best wines for marinating meats are those with relatively high acidity. A young red or white wine from the warm Mediterranean region usually fits the bill.

☐ Leftover wines, in general, are candidates for marinades, as long as they have not developed too much acidity.

☐ Wine's greatest enemy is oxygen, not time. If you drink half of a bottle of wine, pour the leftover liquid into an empty half-bottle, thus minimizing the air space between the wine and cork.

☐ *See also* Sherry.

WINE STAINS

☐ When you accidentally spill red wine on your clothing or tablecloth, attack the problem immediately. The longer you wait, the more the stain will set and the harder your task will be.

☐ First blot up the excess liquid. Then, using warm tap water, rinse as much of the wine out of the fabric as you can. If the stain persists and the fabric permits it, use detergent water.

☐ A fifty-fifty solution of white vinegar and water is an effective stain remover, too, but the advantages of club soda are greatly exaggerated.

☐ If all your efforts fail, turn the stained cloth over to your local dry cleaner who can often perform miracles with the high-tech chemical solutions at his disposal.

WOKS

☐ Rolled carbon steel woks cost much less than the stainless steel units, yet are substantially superior for stir-frying. Reason: Carbon steel distributes the heat of the burner much better than stainless steel. Just be sure that you season the carbon steel wok before you use it and dry it thoroughly immediately after you wash it. Otherwise, it will probably rust.

☐ If you steam as well as stir-fry in a wok, consider having both a carbon and a stainless steel wok. The latter is perfect for steaming, because it won't rust. Moreover, you don't have to be concerned about the poor conductivity of its metal. Reason: The water distributes the heat of the burners before it reaches the food.

☐ When stir-frying, it is essential that you seal in the juices of the food quickly. This won't happen unless the oil is very hot before you add the food to the wok.

WOODENWARE

☐ Don't soak wooden bowls, utensils, and boards in water or clean them in a dishwater.

☐ Woodenware should not be exposed to temperature or humidity extremes; keep them out of the refrigerator and away from the stove.

☐ The wood should be re-oiled when its surface begins to lose its sheen. Apply a generous coating of a non-toxic odorless oil and let stand for 30 minutes. Then wipe off any unabsorbed oil with paper towels.

Y

YEAST

☐ Compressed yeast is more effective than dry yeast, as long as it is fresh (maximum storage life is about 2 weeks in the refrigerator). To test for freshness, first look for the expiration date on the package. Then open and examine the cake: It's over the hill if its surface is blotched or brown. A sour odor is also a negative indicator. When you crumble the yeast, it should break into jagged-edged pieces.

☐ Dry yeast, on the other hand, is more convenient than fresh yeast, because it doesn't need to be refrigerated and has a much longer storage life.

☐ Store dry yeast packets in a sealed jar in a cool, dark place.

☐ To prepare yeast for your recipe, add 1 packet of the dry granular variety or 1 cube of the fresh type to ¼ cup of luke-warm (about 110 degrees) water in a measuring cup. Give the yeast more nourishment by adding ¼ teaspoon of sugar (sub-tract this amount from the recipe). Blend the yeast, sugar, and water, and let the mixture stand for 10 minutes. If it has not actively bubbled by this time, your yeast is impotent and should be discarded.

☐ When in doubt, be conservative rather than liberal in your estimation of how much yeast you need. Too much yeast can give a baked item a yeasty flavor and distorted form.

YOGURT

☐ If you enjoy yogurt with fruit, buy plain yogurt and add your own fresh fruit. Your creation will be more nutritious and less fattening than the commercially made yogurts with fruit.

☐ Most of the fruit-yogurt products on the market are not

dieters' dreams because they are loaded with sugar. Remember, 100 percent natural does not mean sugar-free.

☐ For optimum flavor, buy whole milk rather than skim milk yogurt.

☐ The difference in calories between a cup of the typical whole and skim (low-fat) plain yogurt is less than 50 calories. This saving is hardly worth the sacrifice in flavor and texture. Save your calories elsewhere.

☐ Certain bacteria in yogurt can help digestion. However, don't expect to gain that benefit if you eat frozen yogurt. The freezing process denatures these bacteria.

Z

ZUCCHINI

☐   The most tender and delicately flavored zucchini are the small (young) ones.

☐   Reject zucchini if their skins are cut, coarse, bruised, or dull. The zucchini should not be waxed.

☐   If the zucchini has lost its firmness, it is past its prime.

☐   Enliven salads with diced or thinly sliced zucchini, preferably raw and unpeeled.

☐   Zucchini is a good steamer, but a poor simmerer. It bakes well, if kept moist.

ABOUT THE AUTHOR

Howard Hillman is an avid cook and diner who has traveled to more than one hundred countries, searching for culinary ideas and techniques.

He has written more than twenty books including *Kitchen Science, Great Peasant Dishes of the World, The Cook's Book, The Penguin Book of World Cuisines, The Diner's Guide to Wine, The Gourmet Guide to Beer,* and *The Art of Dining Out.* He is also the author of a nationwide series of critical dining-out guidebooks to seven major cities.

His articles have been published in many distinguished publications including *The New York Times, The Washington Post, Chicago Tribune, Los Angeles Times, The Wall Street Journal, BusinessWeek, Newsweek, Medical World News, The Health Quarterly, Self, The Cook's Magazine,* and *Food & Wine.*

Hillman is a frequent guest on TV and radio news and talk shows around the country.

His general background includes a vice presidency of The American Film Theatre and the presidency of The National Academy of Sports. Howard Hillman is a Harvard Business School graduate and a quality control consultant to major international corporations.